CRAFTY
FAST
FOOD

AND SIDE DISHES

RICE AND GRAINS

These days Britain's shops and supermarkets offer an unrivalled range of grains as fabulous, easy-to-use, alternatives to potatoes and pasta. Rice is perhaps the most obvious but now comes in so many varieties it's almost impossible to list them. Basically they can be divided into three groups: long grain rice, the king of which is Basmati from the foothills of the Himalayas, although most long grain rice is actually grown in America; Oriental rices, often called Thai or Fragrant rice, which have a slightly shorter grain and are stickier when cooked but perfect for Chinese and South-East Asian dishes; and the exotics – wild rice, red rice and other unusual grains. In addition to rice, there is couscous, cracked wheat and polenta. All of these make an excellent background to a whole range of dishes, both Western, whether grills, sautés or stews, and Eastern, such as curries and stir-fries and tajines.

There are also a number of very interesting dishes of which grain is an integral part, instead of just the background, and I've included a number of those recipes here, from North Africa across to France, Spain and over to North America. One of the great things about all these grains is that they are easy to use, usually needing nothing more than a little rinsing before cooking. They are a great alternative to peeling, par-boiling, roasting or mashing (although I am devoted to mashed and roasted potatoes).

Bulgar
CRAFTY INGREDIENT

Bulgar Pilau with Turkish Vegetable Stew Ⓥ

This is one of the great Turkish dishes, with a lovely rich flavour.

time

30 mins

Serves 4

1 tablespoon olive oil
25g (1oz) butter
1 small onion, finely chopped
1 garlic clove
300 g (10 oz) bulgar
grated rind of 1 lemon and ½ the juice

FOR THE SAUCE:
3 tablespoons olive oil
1 large onion, chopped
2 red peppers, cut into 2.5 cm (1 inch) pieces
700 g bottle fresh Italian tomato sauce
1 tablespoon sun-dried tomato purée
1 teaspoon chilli sauce or purée
salt and freshly ground black pepper
1 tablespoon chopped fresh or frozen parsley

BULGAR OR BURGHUL

● This is wholegrain wheat which has been roughly cracked until the grains are almost the size of a rice grain. It can be used in a variety of ways, either in a pilau like this one, or as a stuffing for chicken or pheasant, or indeed any bird, as it soaks up the flavours extraordinarily well.

● When not cooked, but soaked for 30 minutes in water and then drained, it makes an excellent salad. Mixed with lots of chopped parsley, mint, tomatoes and onions, it makes the famous Middle Eastern dish Tabbouleh.

Heat the tablespoon of olive oil and the butter in a saucepan, add the onion and garlic and fry gently until translucent. Add the bulgar and stir until coated with the mixture. Pour in 450 ml (15 fl oz) water, the lemon rind and juice and stir again. Bring to the boil, then simmer very gently over the lowest heat until the liquid has been absorbed. Remove from the heat, cover with a tea-towel or kitchen paper, put the lid on and leave to stand for 5 minutes.

Meanwhile, make the sauce. Heat the oil in a saucepan, add the onion and fry for 2–3 minutes, until softened. Stir in the red peppers, tomato sauce, tomato purée and chilli sauce and season generously with salt and pepper. Simmer gently, half covered, for 5 minutes, stirring every 2–3 minutes.

To serve put the pilau in a warmed serving bowl and the sauce in a separate bowl, sprinkled with parsley.

RICE AND GRAINS

57

Outdoor Wines

Y ou've picked the perfect day: the picnic hamper (a coolbox to you and me!) is packed with goodies, or perhaps it's time to fire up the barbecue? Glyndebourne gourmet, clingfilm wrapped sandwich, sizzling steak – any food is going to taste twice as good outdoors as in. The open air also does something wonderful to the taste of wine. Lazy, sun-soaked, outdoor days scream for easy-drinking, cheap and cheerful wines that shouldn't be taken too seriously. Simplicity and fun is the secret – wines that are good for drinking on their own as we chatter and lounge, as well as to sip while the sausages spit.

Pretty pink rosés are quintessential summer sippers that don't demand much concentration. It doesn't really matter which country they come from, though there are much more exciting examples than Rosé Anjou or Mateus. What is important is freshness, so choose the youngest you can find and serve it nicely-chilled.

For red wine lovers, fruity, happy-go-lucky, red Lambrusco, with its snappy acidity and dash of cherry fruit, is a peerless sweet and sour happy juice, partnering both sweet and savoury foods surprisingly well. Another marvellous frizzy outdoor wine is the juicy, sweet, yet meadow-fresh, Asti Spumante, served as cold as possible.

There are no wines in the world, however, which more brilliantly reflect the scents and flavours of an English summer day than the Riesling Spätleses of Germany's Mosel valley. They have an exhilarating green snap to their flourishing sweet fruit, a lovely streak of lime and lemon acidity, all wrapped in a dewy perfume redolent of wild flowers, honeysuckle and hedgerow. Add to this a flicker of soft gentleness and even the merest hint of a sparkle and you have the most sublime outdoor wine.

A picnic packing list reminder...!

E. M. Forster would have us believe that no picnic is complete without a mackintosh square. A damp bottom, though, is nothing compared with the sudden discovery that you've left the corkscrew behind!

Smoked Turkey
CRAFTY INGREDIENT

SLICED SMOKED TURKEY

● This is an American import, although in style these days rather than in substance. It consists of lightly smoked breast of turkey that's sliced in wafer thin slices, usually in a square or round shape, and packed into plastic trays. It needs unrolling quite carefully but is surprisingly tasty.

● It's good as a part of a mixed hors d'oeuvre, very good in sandwiches, particularly with light mustard pickle and maybe some dill gherkins, and excellent as a filling for dishes such as omelettes.

Stuffed Peppers with Smoked Turkey and Couscous

Sweet peppers have become an almost everyday vegetable in Britain in the last ten years. They originally came from Mexico but have been developed in their present form by the Dutch who have bred them even bigger and sweeter. They make perfect vehicles for stuffing, as when you remove the seeds you have a large, boat-shaped container. This filling is very easy, using ready prepared couscous, the cracked wheat from the Middle East, which cooks very much like rice. If you wish, you can substitute vegetarian cheese for the smoked turkey.

time

30 mins

Serves 4

25 g (1oz) butter
25 g (1 oz) vegetable oil
100 g/4 oz onion, finely chopped
225 g (8 oz) couscous
50 g (2 oz) sultanas
½ teaspoon allspice
½ teaspoon ground cumin
100 g (4 oz) wafer thin smoked turkey , shredded
2 large red peppers, halved and seeded
2 large green peppers, halved and seeded

Pre-heat the oven to 200°C/400°F/Gas 6.

Melt the butter and oil in a frying pan, add the onion and fry gently. Meanwhile, measure the couscous in a jug, then mix in a bowl with its own volume of water (about 300 ml/10 fl oz). Leave to stand for about 5 minutes, until the water has been absorbed. Add the couscous to the onion with the sultanas and the spices and heat together for 5–6 minutes, stirring occasionally, until the couscous is hot. Stir in the shredded turkey. Place the pepper halves on a baking tray and stuff with the couscous mixture. Bake in the oven for 15–20 minutes, until the peppers are tender and the stuffing slightly golden.

RICE AND GRAINS

Couscous with Quick Vegetable Sauce Ⓥ

This is a very simple, quick way of cooking couscous.

time

30 mins

Serves 4

350 g (12 oz) couscous
25 ml (1 fl oz) olive oil
25 g (1oz) butter

FOR THE SAUCE:
2 tablespoons olive oil
1 onion, finely chopped
2 teaspoons garlic purée
1½ teaspoons chilli powder
½ teaspoon ground coriander
½ teaspoon ground cumin
2 tablespoons tomato purée
450 g (1 lb) mixed frozen vegetables, including cauliflower,
    carrots and peppers

Put the couscous in a bowl, stir in 600 ml (1 pint) water and leave to soak for about 5 minutes, until the water has been absorbed. Stir in the olive oil. Turn the couscous into a colander and stand over a saucepan containing 2.5 cm (1 inch) of boiling water. Cover and bring to the boil.

Meanwhile, make the sauce. Heat the olive oil in a saucepan, add the onion and 1 teaspoon garlic purée and fry gently for 2–3 minutes. Add ½ teaspoon chilli powder, the coriander and the tomato purée and continue to cook gently for another 5 minutes. Add the frozen vegetables and enough hot water to just cover. Bring to the boil, then simmer for about 5 minutes.

When the couscous is hot, stir in the butter and arrange on a warmed serving plate. Remove the vegetables from the pan with a slotted spoon and pile them into the middle. Pour over a little of the sauce. Add the remaining teaspoon of chilli and garlic to the remaining sauce to make a potent seasoning called harissa. Serve this separately.

MIXED FROZEN VEGETABLES

● These make an extremely useful addition to all kinds of casseroles and stews with the main advantage being that all the hard work of preparation has been taken out. They come under a variety of names, often called 'stew pack vegetables' or 'exotic frozen vegetables', depending on the ingredients.
● The key thing is not to cook them for too long and preferably not just in water. They go well in casseroles and, once blanched in boiling water, make an excellent addition to a gratin, and ought not to be despised for the making of a quick vegetable soup.

RICE AND GRAINS

60

Fried Rice with Prawns

This is a simple, quick Chinese recipe making use of cooked rice. If you haven't got any ready, it's worth cooking some just to make this dish which has a light, bright freshness to it. Fried rice in China is used as a snack (like we might have a fast food takeaway), rather than as part of a complete meal but I don't think we need to respect that convention too much. It makes an excellent lunch or even light dinner dish, particularly with a bowl of good soup to start with.

time

15 mins

TIGER PRAWNS

● These are the large, warm-water, tropical prawns that have bands on their shells, rather reminiscent of tiger stripes. You can buy them raw or cooked, frozen or chilled, but my recommendation for this dish is shelled and cooked.
● Raw, they make a marvellous basis for a *Thai Prawn Curry* (see p. 101) and, although it's a bit extravagant, they make a smashing prawn cocktail.

Serves 4

2 tablespoons vegetable oil

2 garlic cloves or 1 teaspoon garlic purée

15 g (½ oz) chopped ginger or 1 teaspoon ginger purée

1 bunch spring onions, chopped

100 g (4 oz) frozen peas

2 eggs, beaten

2 tablespoons light soy sauce

225 g (8 oz) cooked, shelled tiger prawns

350 g (12 oz) cold cooked rice

In a large frying pan or wok, heat the oil until just below smoking point. Add the garlic, ginger and spring onions and stir-fry for 1 minute. Add the frozen peas and stir-fry for another minute. Add the beaten eggs and scramble the mixture until the eggs are just set, stirring and tossing all the time. Pour the soy sauce in around the edge of the pan so that it runs down into the mixture, and toss for a few moments. Add the prawns and rice, and toss until the rice is hot and the ingredients are mixed together. Serve hot.

RICE AND GRAINS

Tiger Prawns

CRAFTY INGREDIENT

Paella

This is a really quick paella which nevertheless manages to capture some of the authentic flavours of Spain. Do use real saffron. Even in Spain they sell imitation colouring but it simply doesn't have the same flavour or colour.

time

30 mins

Serves 4

2 tablespoons olive oil

2 boneless chicken breasts, skinned and each cut into 4 pieces

2 large onions, finely chopped

salt and freshly ground black pepper

275 g (10 oz) long grain rice

750 ml (1¼ pints) chicken stock

1 packet saffron threads or powdered saffron

350 g (12 oz) mixed exotic, oriental frozen vegetables, including
    sweetcorn and peppers, thawed

350 g (12 oz) seafood/seafood cocktail mix without dressing

175 g (6 oz) cherry tomatoes, halved

chopped fresh parsley, to garnish

lemon wedges, to serve

Heat the oil in a large frying-pan, add the chicken pieces and fry for 2–3 minutes. Add the onions and fry for a further 2–3 minutes. Season generously with salt and pepper, then add the rice, stirring well to ensure that the rice is well coated in the oil. Pour in 600 ml (1 pint) of the chicken stock, bring to the boil and simmer gently, uncovered, for about 10 minutes, until most of the liquid has been absorbed.

Meanwhile, if using saffron threads, put them into a dessert spoon and crush with the back of a teaspoon. Add the saffron threads or powder to the remaining chicken stock and stir gently. Set aside to soak.

Before all the liquid in the rice has been absorbed, add the thawed vegetables, seafood, tomatoes and the saffron flavoured stock. Stir gently. Cover and simmer for 10 minutes. Remove the lid, allow to stand for 2–3 minutes, sprinkle over a little chopped parsley to serve with lemon wedges.

CHILLED SEAFOOD MIX

● This is a marvellous development which includes, in one packet, shelled prawns, mussels, squid and, if you're lucky, some crab or perhaps sliced crab sticks. You can buy it frozen as well as chilled.

● It's designed to be used in a kind of seafood cocktail but is also excellent lightly cooked, as in this recipe.

● It's good in Thai fish soups and is an excellent base for an Italian seafood casserole with one or two pieces of chunky fish, such as salmon, cod and hake, added to the rich tomato, onion and garlic sauce.

RICE AND GRAINS

Red Hot Rice Salad Ⓥ

This is a dish that really needs to go with other dishes. Certainly a green and cooling salad would be a good idea. It's particularly good with grilled fish and grilled light meats. In keeping with its name, it needs to be served slightly warm.

time

30 mins

Serves 4

275 g (10 oz) red rice

225 g (8 oz) tomatoes, finely chopped

225 g (8 oz) onions, finely chopped

1 red pepper, seeded and finely chopped

2 finger-sized red chilli peppers, seeded and finely chopped

1 tablespoon snipped fresh or frozen chives, to garnish

FOR THE DRESSING:

50 ml (2 fl oz) red wine vinegar

150 ml (5 fl oz) olive oil

½ teaspoon salt

½ teaspoon sugar

2 teaspoons sun-dried tomato purée

salt and freshly ground black pepper

Cook the rice according to the instructions on the packet. Meanwhile, mix together the tomatoes, onions, red pepper and chillies. (After preparing the chillies, wash your hands and knife carefully before touching your face, particularly your eyes.)

To make the dressing, whisk together all the ingredients. When the rice is cooked, drain into a colander and run under cold water until it's cool but not totally chilled. Allow to drain again, then mix with the vegetable mixture. Season generously with salt and a little pepper, pour over the dressing, to taste, and toss together until well mixed. Sprinkle over the chives and leave to marinate, if time, for 10–30 minutes before serving.

RICE AND GRAINS

RED RICE

● This is a real newcomer on the market, brought in by one of the speciality food companies that has recently emerged to satisfy the gourmet market. It originally comes from the Carmargue in the South-West of France and the Rhône Delta where the famous cowboys and white bulls and flamingoes are to be found. Apparently it is grown in a very small local area and has recently been developed as a major crop.

● It can be eaten in most of the ways that conventional rice can. It cooks to a pinkish colour and has a good nutty flavour and texture. It's particularly good in dishes which set off its colour, like this salad, or perhaps as a spectacular bed for some pure white, cooked fish.

Lemon Garlic Rice Ⓥ

The flavours of lemon and garlic go well with most dishes, particularly with fish. However, if you're a vegetarian this is a marvellous dish on its own, perhaps with some chutneys, and a cucumber and yoghurt salad.

Serves 4

1 tablespoon vegetable oil
25g (1 oz) butter
2 teaspoons garlic purée
250g (8 oz) Basmati rice
juice and grated rind of 1 lemon
salt and freshly ground black pepper
a few coriander leaves, to garnish

Heat the oil and butter in a saucepan, add the garlic purée and rice and fry for 1–2 minutes until the rice becomes translucent. Pour the lemon juice into a measuring jug and top up with water to 450ml (15 fl oz). Add the grated lemon rind and season with salt and pepper. Add the lemon-flavoured water to the pan. Bring to the boil and simmer for 15 minutes. Remove from the heat, cover with a tea-towel or a double thickness of kitchen paper, then a lid, and leave for 5 minutes. Serve garnished with coriander.

GARLIC PUREE

● Suddenly the kind of garlic purées that I only used to be able to buy in Singaporean food markets have appeared in jars on my local supermarket shelves, and very welcome too. Lots of different firms make them but look for the ones whose ingredients are only garlic, salt and perhaps a drop of oil to help preserve the mixture.

● You can use it anywhere you'd use fresh garlic, in stir-fries or curries, spread on meat before you grill it, mixed into sauces for pasta or spread on pizzas before you bake them. It's one of the most versatile ingredients and I always keep a jar in my fridge, though it doesn't seem to last very long.

Garlic Purée
CRAFTY INGREDIENT

RICE AND GRAINS

Polenta with Wild Mushrooms

Polenta is sometimes described as cornmeal porridge, which does it rather less than justice. It's closer in fact to cornmeal mashed potatoes as it's made in quite a rich and flavoursome way in Northern and Eastern Italy. There they almost always serve it with a rich stew. Here is a vegetarian version, based on mushrooms, of which there is such a large variety these days. The classic way to serve it is to make a nest of the polenta when it's cooked and pour the mushroom (or any other stew) into the centre. If the polenta gets cold, by the way, it's very nice the next day grilled or lightly fried in some olive oil.

time

25 mins

Serves 4

225 g (8 oz) fine polenta

I teaspoon salt

50 g (2oz) butter, plus extra to serve

50 g (2oz) freshly grated Parmesan cheese

FOR THE STEW:

3 tablespoons olive oil

225 g (8 oz) onions, finely chopped

450 g (I lb) assorted wild or exotic mushrooms such as oyster, shiitake, and/or chestnut mushrooms, thickly sliced

I garlic clove, finely chopped

salt and freshly ground black pepper

120 ml (4 fl oz) red grape juice

I teaspoon chopped fresh or frozen oregano

I teaspoon chopped fresh or frozen thyme

I tablespoon chopped fresh or frozen parsley

chopped fresh parsley, to garnish

MIXED WILD MUSHROOMS

● We've begun to 'grow' wild mushrooms, or their close relatives, rather well in recent years and a wide variety exists. Chestnut mushrooms look like our old-style mushrooms but are a chestnut brown colour and have much more density and strength of flavour. Oyster mushrooms are flat and shaped like an unopened oyster. They have no fishy flavour at all but a good, rich mushroom flavour and an interesting texture. Shiitake are a Japanese mushroom which grow on wooden logs and are quite dark in colour and firm, with a rich flavour.

● They can be used in all the ways conventional mushrooms can but are particularly good in soups, salads and stews.

In a large saucepan bring 900 ml (1½ pints) water and the salt to the boil. Gradually add the polenta, letting it run through your fingers in a thin stream, stirring constantly to prevent lumps forming. Simmer for 10–15 minutes, until the mixture comes away from the sides of the pan, stirring frequently.

Meanwhile, prepare the stew. Heat the oil in a large frying pan, add the onions and fry for about 5 minutes until softened. Add the mushrooms and garlic and season well with salt and pepper. Half cover and simmer for 10–15 minutes.

When the polenta is cooked, stir in the butter and the Parmesan cheese. Remove from the heat and leave to stand for 5–6 minutes.

When most of the mushroom juices have evaporated from the stew, add the grape juice and the herbs. Bring to the boil, stirring vigorously, and cook for about 3 minutes.

Serve the polenta on warmed serving plates in a nest and sprinkle on a little more cheese or add a little more butter if it's too thick or dry. Spoon the mushroom stew and its sauce into the middle and sprinkle with chopped parsley to garnish.

QUICK COOK POLENTA

● A 10–15 minute version of the traditional polenta or cornmeal porridge (the original takes an hour to cook). It's really a kind of north Italian mashed potato which can be enriched by butter, cheese, herbs and sautés. When it's cold, it sets so you can slice and grill or fry it to accompany grilled meats and vegetables, or as a base for spicey toppings.

Wild Mushrooms
CRAFTY INGREDIENT

CHEESE AND EGGS

Cheese and eggs are the original convenience foods. There is, for example, simply nothing more convenient than an egg, and people across the world have developed an extraordinary number of different ways to cook them. Perhaps one of my favourites is a Thai recipe for Son-in-Law Eggs, the idea being that Thai mothers-in-law are so fond of their daughters' husbands that they make them this special dish from hard-boiled duck eggs. We tend to limit our ambitions to those dishes that are served at breakfast time, scrambled, poached, fried or boiled, although to me there are few things more comforting than soft-boiled eggs and wholemeal soldiers served with a pot of really good tea. But the opportunity to make more exciting dishes, such as omelettes and exotic scrambled eggs, should not be missed. They are amongst the quickest dishes that it's possible to produce.

Cheeses too are instant food, whether cut into chunks, grated over dishes and flashed under the grill, or mixed into sauces. It's interesting how delicious cheeses designed primarily for cooking, like Parmesan, are when eaten raw. Just try a really ripe pear, a chunk of Parmesan and some Italian bread to discover how wonderfully simple eating can be.

Eggs are also the basis for some of the most refined cooking in the world, often combined with cheese. If the thought of making a soufflé appalls you, relax, this is an effortless method. Please don't let on how easy it is.

Do be adventurous. Try blue cheese in one of your cheese sauces; it's marvellous on vegetables such as broccoli. One of the tangy cheeses, such as Lancashire or a mature Cheddar or Gouda, coarsely grated into a salad of crisp and bitter leaves makes a wonderful combination. Try the soft cheeses, particularly the ones from Italy, such as Ricotta, with its dry and low-fat texture, to Mascarpone, the full-fat, almost sweet cheese cream that's used in puddings as much as savoury dishes. They also mix well into sauces, add a fabulous texture to desserts and bake well in sweet and savoury tarts. The only limit is your imagination.

● The ultimate convenience food, the supply of which has vastly improved in Britain in the last five years. Public concern for both animal welfare and human health has led to an enormous expansion of high-quality eggs as opposed to battery production. Free range, organic and barn eggs are now the dominant products in the market place and the food of the chickens is a matter of much concern.

● Only free range, organic chickens are likely to have the run of a farmyard in the way that we might like to imagine, but the quality of life of the others have greatly improved, and so too have the eggs, with firm shells, bright golden yolks, not derived from colourings, and great flavour.

Italian Frittata

Devoted as I am to French omelettes, it's important to remember that there are other kinds too. The Italian Frittata, while cooked flat, not rolled, and usually containing some vegetables or other ingredients, is also the antithesis of the Spanish omelette, which is always cooked at least 4 cm (1½ inches) thick if possible. Individual, tea plate sized, Frittata make a wonderful beginning to an Italian rustic meal. They are also a great standby as a snack or a light lunch. You can cook large ones and divide them but I always think individual Frittata are the best. If you want to make a large one, multiply the ingredients here by four.

time

10 mins

Serves 1

2 tablespoons olive oil
50 g (2 oz) courgette, thinly sliced
2 eggs, beaten
salt and freshly ground black pepper
25 g (1 oz) freshly grated Parmesan cheese
1 teaspoon snipped fresh or frozen chives

Pre-heat the grill. Heat the oil in a 13 cm (5 inch) frying pan and quickly fry the courgettes on both sides for about 1½ minutes. Add the eggs and stir with a fork, trying to keep the courgettes as flat as possible, until most of the egg is cooked. When the omelette is set on the bottom, season lightly with salt and sprinkle the Parmesan cheese, then the chives, on top. Slide the pan under the hot grill for 45 seconds to 1 minute, until the top of the omelette just starts to bubble. Serve immediately on warmed plates with plenty of pepper.

CHEESE AND EGGS

Eggs
CRAFTY INGREDIENT

Quick Cheese Soufflé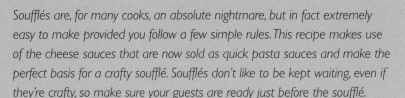

Soufflés are, for many cooks, an absolute nightmare, but in fact extremely easy to make provided you follow a few simple rules. This recipe makes use of the cheese sauces that are now sold as quick pasta sauces and make the perfect basis for a crafty soufflé. Soufflés don't like to be kept waiting, even if they're crafty, so make sure your guests are ready just before the soufflé.

time

30 mins

Serves 4

25 g (1 oz) butter

3 eggs, separated

225 ml (8 oz) fresh cheese sauce for pasta

50 g (2 oz) grated Parmesan cheese

salt and freshly ground black pepper

Pre-heat the oven to 200°C/400°F/Gas 6. Grease a 600 ml (1 pint) soufflé dish with some of the butter.

Beat the egg yolks into the cheese sauce and heat gently in a non-stick saucepan. Add the remaining butter and remove from the heat as soon as the butter has melted.

Whisk the egg whites until stiff, then carefully fold in the cheese sauce with 2 tablespoons of the Parmesan cheese. Pour the mixture into the prepared dish and sprinkle with the remaining cheese.

Bake in the oven for 20–25 minutes. It should be golden and crispy on the top, well risen but with a hint of softness in the centre. Serve it immediately on warmed plates.

READY-GRATED PARMESAN CHEESE

● Although recipes tell you to use whole pieces of Parmesan cheese and grate it freshly, and although this is undoubtedly the best way to do it, a large tub of ready grated Parmesan cheese in the fridge is still an enormously useful standby.

● Use it as a topping for gratins, over pasta dishes, to add a little extra flavouring to meatballs or meat loaf mixtures, and, not least, in soups – minestrone or any vegetable soup that will be improved by the addition of a tablespoon of salty, crumbly Parmesan cheese.

Parmesan

CRAFTY INGREDIENT

Quick Eggs Benedict

Eggs Benedict is an American dish, so legend has it, which has been much maligned by cheap and shoddy imitations. In its original form its layers of toast, tongue, poached egg and hollandaise sauce are stunningly delicious. If that sounds daunting, the ingredients now available make it more a matter of compilation than of cooking. It's a super supper dish that can be preceded by a little soup, then followed by some fruit and cheese. It is also excellent for a light lunch.

time

15 mins

Serves 4

4 large slices of wholemeal bread

50 g (2 oz) butter

4 slices of cooked tongue

4 eggs

1 teaspoon vinegar

8 tablespoons ready made hollandaise sauce

parsley sprigs, to garnish

Pre-heat the grill. Toast the bread, then spread lightly with the butter. Place a slice of tongue on each and place on individual plates.

Poach the eggs. The crafty way of doing this is to bring about 4 cm (1½ inches) water and the vinegar to the boil in a frying pan. Break the eggs, separately, on to a saucer and then slip them into the pan, stirring the water with a spoon into a little whirlpool. Cook for about 1½ minutes, until lightly set, then lift out with a slotted spoon. Drain well and place on to the tongue.

Meanwhile, gently heat the hollandaise sauce in a non-stick saucepan, stirring occasionally, until hot, but do not allow it to boil. When all the eggs are poached, pour the hollandaise sauce over the eggs and serve immediately, garnished with a parsley sprig.

READY-MADE HOLLANDAISE SAUCE

● This is an enormously good standby but make sure the ingredients listed on the jar include eggs, butter and lemon juice and/or vinegar and not much else.

● There are a number of makes; I tend to find the French varieties the best.

● Hollandaise sauce is lovely with poached salmon or with asparagus. It's also good on more mundane vegetables like new potatoes and baby carrots.

● If you can find blood oranges you can stir a couple of tablespoons of their red juice into some Hollandaise sauce to make Maltaise sauce, which is often eaten with fish on Malta.

CHEESE AND EGGS

MOZZARELLA CHEESE

● Mozzarella cheese is made properly in Southern Italy with buffalo milk. Although it's creamy white and looks quite innocent it has a very substantial flavour which cooking seems to bring out best. It's also an extremely stringy cheese, especially when hot, and as well as being a key ingredient of pizzas, is used a lot in other cooked dishes where the melting quality is important.

● It's often served mixed with baked rice dishes, particularly in Sicily and the Campagna, and deep-fried between slices of bread to make a famous snack known as Mozzarella in Carrozza (Mozzarella in a Carriage).

Rice, Pesto and Mozzarella Balls

In Sicily there's a great tradition of selling rice balls, very similar to these, in the street as fast food. They range from marble size to orange size, which are very substantial and, frankly, quite difficult to handle in the street, particularly as they're full of hot, stringy Mozzarella cheese. Made in smaller sizes, however, they make an unusual first course and are also good as cocktail snacks if you're prepared to do some deep-frying just before your guests arrive.

time

15 mins

Makes 12

175 g (6 oz) cooked rice
2 tablespoons pesto sauce
2 eggs, separated
100 g (4 oz) Mozzarella cheese, grated
vegetable oil, for deep-frying

Put the cooked rice in a bowl and add the pesto and the egg yolks. Mix thoroughly, add the Mozzarella cheese and mix again. Roll the mixture into 12 even-sized balls. Whisk the egg whites until they just hold their shape. Heat the oil for frying. Roll the rice balls in the egg white and then carefully drop into the hot oil. Cook until they are slightly puffed, golden and have risen to the surface. Do not let them cook any longer than this. Drain carefully on kitchen paper and serve immediately, remembering that the insides are still likely to be very hot even when the outsides have cooled a little.

Mozzarella

CRAFTY INGREDIENT

Wine and Cheese

When was the last time you drank sweet, late-picked, German Riesling with cheese?! Well, yes, it's more usual to associate red wine with cheese and it can be a delectable combination. However, white wines are often far better partners, especially those with nuances of sweetness.

The Cheeseboard

Different cheeses do demand different wines, so how do you get around the tricky problem of the cheeseboard? Simply forget it! Instead, serve just one cheese alongside its best wine partner – although this could involve you in having rather a lot of bottles on the go at once!

BLUE CHEESE

Roquefort and Stilton Sauternes (the classic), Old Tawny Port, Botrytis-affected Australian Sémillon, Moscatel de Valencia, Barsac, German Beerenauslese

Gorgonzola German Trockenbeerenauslese, Hungarian Tokaji, Dry Muscat d'Alsace

Danish Blue Best to avoid wine. Actually, now I think of it, best to avoid the cheese.

SOFT CHEESE

Brie and Camembert These often have a slight tang of ammonia that clashes violently with wine. Chianti Classico can work with Brie (but don't serve an expensive one) while Camembert can take a gutsier red – try something from the south of France, such as Fitou or Corbières.

Boursin Anything from the Sauvignon Blanc grape

Feta Alsace Riesling

Munster Alsace Gewürztraminer

Port-Salut Côtes-du-Rhône, light Italian reds such as Bardolino,

HARD CHEESE

Caerphilly Red Rioja – the most expensive you can afford, mature claret

Cheddar Claret, Salice Salentino, Châteauneuf-du-Pape , Lebanese Château Musar

Cheshire Californian Cabernet Sauvignon, Sauternes

Double Gloucester Montepulciano d'Abruzzo

Edam Basic Bordeaux or Cabernet Sauvignon

Emmental and Gruyère Californian Sauvignon Blanc, Gewürztraminer d'Alsace, Barbera d'Alba, Australian Shiraz, red Burgundy, Californian Zinfandel

Lancashire Chianti, Sauternes

Red Leicester Rioja, Australian Shiraz

Wensleydale Sauternes, German Riesling Spätlese

Goats' Cheese Sancerre, New Zealand Sauvignon Blanc

SMOKED CHEESE

Sauternes

● Unlike most cheese slices
which are processed, the
Norwegian varieties are cut
from the whole cheese and
therefore retain their flavour
and texture far better.

● As well as their obvious and
delicious use in sandwiches
(I like them with salami and
smoked turkey), they also
make a very good quick
topping for a gratin, spread out
over the vegetables or other
ingredients in a single layer and
sprinkled with a few
breadcrumbs and then grilled.

● They are traditionally served
in a Norwegian version of the
cold buffet or Smörgasbord.

Scandinavian Rarebit

This is a super quick way of making a variation of that great standby, Welsh Rarebit, an oft-decried dish when poorly made. This version uses cheese slices but not everyday processed cheese slices, so flavour and quality are not at all impaired. It is terrific for high tea and good if you're serving a traditional savoury meal.

time

10 mins

Serves 4

4 large, thick slices of white crusty bread
50 g (2 oz) butter
1 tablespoon Dijon mustard
150 g (5 oz) Norwegian Jarlsberg cheese slices (about 10 slices)
freshly ground black pepper
4 teaspoons lime mango chutney

Pre-heat the grill. Lightly toast the bread, then spread with butter to the edges. Spread the Dijon mustard over the toast and place several slices of the cheese on each, making sure they are right to the edge. Season with pepper and spread the mango chutney on top. Cook under the grill for 2–3 minutes, until the cheese has melted and is bubbling. Serve immediately, remembering that hot cheese is very hot.

CHEESE AND EGGS

Norwegian
Cheese Slices
CRAFTY INGREDIENT

Scrambled Chilli Eggs ⓥ

This is a Los Angeles invention although I suspect it probably has many originators in different parts of the United States. The technique of scrambling the eggs in a wide frying pan, rather than a deep saucepan, produces a terrific texture and the powerful impact of the flavourings makes it more a brunch than a breakfast dish.

time

5 mins

Serves 4

25 ml (I fl oz) vegetable oil (not olive oil)

50 g (2 oz) butter

8 eggs, beaten

I teaspoon celery salt

50 g (2 oz) Cheddar cheese, grated

I tablespoon chilli sauce

4 tablespoons tomato ketchup

In a 25 cm (10 inch) frying pan, heat the oil and melt the butter. When it has stopped sizzling, pour in the eggs and season immediately with the celery salt. Using a fish slice or a palette knife, cook the eggs by pushing them, from the edge to the centre, into folds, across the pan, until softly set. When the eggs are cooked, sprinkle with the cheese.

Stir the chilli sauce into the ketchup and drizzle over the eggs in an attractive pattern before serving.

CELERY SALT

● Celery salt is just one of a number of seasoned salts that are available on our spice shelves. The flavour is derived from the seed rather than from the stalk of the plant.

● It is marvellous in tomato juice cocktails or sprinkled over vegetable soups, and gives an unexpected lift to casserole dishes.

● Other flavoured salts, apart from garlic, now include rather exotic varieties like Moroccan stir-fry and Indonesian flavoured salts. They are all interesting and should be used with some discretion but don't be afraid to experiment.

CHEESE AND EGGS

Pulses, the collective name given to dried beans, peas and lentils, have developed a slightly unfortunate image, in that they tend to be associated with boring vegetarian food. It is estimated that 3–4 per cent of men and 5–6 per cent of women in Britain are effectively full-time vegetarians and a much larger number, more than double, have vegetarian inclinations. If the reputation of vegetarian food has been maligned, so too has that of beans and pulses. In fact, they form the basis of a most delicious and substantial style of cooking for many dishes and in many parts of the world. Middle Eastern, Egyptian, Greek and Turkish cooking rely enormously on a range of beans and pulses, both fresh and dried, to make everything from deep-fried Falafels to creamy dips and rich stews. It's that range of recipes that I've tried to reflect here.

The great virtue of beans and pulses is that they absorb and carry flavours brilliantly. Sometimes those tastes are very simple, such as the strong tomato flavouring of Boston Baked Beans, and sometimes they're quite complicated and sophisticated, as with the vegetable spiced dals of the Indian subcontinent.

Apart from the delicious tastes and interesting textures, pulses have one or two added advantages. One, and perhaps the most important nutritionally, is that they are a tremendous source of fibre, which is held to be so important in our diet these days. In addition, they are a high protein food as well as high fibre so there's no cheaper way to produce a balanced diet than to use plenty of pulses. The third characteristic that makes them particularly convenient is that they can be canned so successfully. You can, and I often do, buy dried beans, chick peas and lentils, and start from scratch, soaking and then cooking them, but that can be a time-consuming process even though it's often very satisfying. However, almost every imaginable kind of bean, lentil and pulse is available these days in canned form, with no loss of flavour or texture.

BEANS AND PULSES

Falafels

Here is another way of using chick peas to produce a marvellous and hugely popular vegetarian 'meat' ball. They're eaten all over the Middle East, Turkey and these days occasionally in Greece. They're both street food and restaurant food and can be bought in most markets or souks nestling in warm pitta bread with a sauce made of yoghurt and garlic or sesame seeds poured over. They're a particular speciality in Cairo where they're also made with broad beans. They can be shallow- or deep-fried, in which case they tend to be a little rounder. Quick Hummus (see p. 34), hot pitta bread and salad are the perfect accompaniments.

time

20 mins

Makes 18

420 g (14½ oz) can chick peas

50 g (2 oz) onions

1 egg, beaten

½ teaspoon turmeric

½ teaspoon paprika

1 tablespoon finely chopped fresh or frozen parsley

½ teaspoon baking powder

25 g (1 oz) fresh bread crumbs

vegetable oil, for deep- or shallow-frying

Rinse the chick peas under cold water and drain well. Put in a food processor with all the other ingredients and blend until smooth. If necessary, add 1 tablespoon water but the mixture should be thick and firm like dough.

Heat the oil for frying. Take out 1 tablespoon of the mixture at a time, and form into little balls. If you are deep-frying, drop each ball carefully into the hot oil. If you are shallow-frying, squash each ball into a thick 3.5 cm (1½ inch) wide patty before adding to the oil. Fry for 5–6 minutes, until golden brown and crispy on the outside.

CANNED CHICK PEAS

● These are a really useful ingredient, as using dried chick peas you are at least 8 hours away from eating.

● Apart from making Falafels they make a very good, slightly coarse-grained *Spinach and Chick Pea Soup* (see p. 17), are an essential part of Couscous, and make an excellent dhal known as Channa Dhal to eat with Indian curries. You cook tomatoes, onions and spices together first, add the chick peas and simmer for a few minutes.

BEANS AND PULSES

CANNED KIDNEY BEANS IN CHILLI SAUCE

● Increasingly these days canned vegetables come ready flavoured and chilli kidney beans are extremely useful.

● The amount of chilli varies from manufacturer to manufacturer so it's as well to check how much there is before adding any other flavouring yourself.

● Apart from Chilli Con Carne they make an excellent basis for a meatless version which should include a chopped red and green pepper and half a head of celery to replace the meat. Alternatively, you could use some of the newly developed vegetarian protein mince that's very good at absorbing flavours in its own right.

● The beans also make a good accompanying dish if you're making other Mexican food, like Turkey in Molé Poblano Sauce or grilled spiced fish, in which case the beans just need heating through and serving in a bowl.

Quick Chilli Con Carne

Chilli Con Carne has become rather a cliché in Britain, appearing on every pub menu and in many fast food places in a rather inferior version. In America they get very picky about Chilli Con Carne as it's really a Texan dish, rather than a Mexican one, but leaving that kind of obsession apart, it is very warming and cheering and can be made quite authentically using canned beans. It's best served with plenty of plainly cooked rice and either a salad or sweetcorn cooked with onions and chopped peppers.

Serves 4

time

25 mins

1 tablespoon vegetable oil
450 g (1 lb) lean minced beef
225 g (8 oz) onions, finely chopped
1 garlic clove, crushed
½ teaspoon ground cumin
½ teaspoon ground cinnamon
salt and freshly ground black pepper
420 g (14½ oz) can kidney beans in chilli sauce
2 tablespoons tomato purée
1 teaspoon chilli sauce (if necessary)

Heat the oil in a frying pan, add the beef and fry until browned and separated, stirring frequently. Add the onions, garlic and the spices and season generously with salt and pepper. Fry gently for a further 4–5 minutes, until the onions begin to soften. Stir in the beans, then taste and check the amount of chilli in the sauce before adding the additional chilli. Simmer the sauce for 5 minutes. Stir in the tomato purée and add about 100ml (4 fl oz) water, if necessary, to produce a thick but not rigid mixture. Simmer gently for a further 6–10 minutes before serving.

BEANS AND PULSES

Kidney Beans
CRAFTY INGREDIENT

Thai Tofu with Bean Sprouts Ⓥ

Thai flavourings are wonderfully sharp and clear and powerful, often very tangy and frequently extremely hot with chilli. This one isn't hot but has all the other virtues. Fortunately tofu (bean curd) is such a popular ingredient in Britain these days, particularly with vegetarians and vegans, that it's widely available in most of its different forms in supermarkets. Serve this dish on its own with rice or as part of a large Thai meal.

time

10 mins

Serves 4

2 tablespoons vegetable oil

5 cm (1 inch) piece of fresh ginger or 1 teaspoon ginger purée

1 garlic clove or 1 teaspoon garlic purée

225 g (8 oz) packet smoked tofu, cut into 1 cm (½ inch) cubes

1 bunch spring onions, cut into 1 cm (½ inch) lengths

juice of 1 lime

½ teaspoon chilli purée or sauce

4 tablespoons soy sauce

200 g (7 oz) bean sprouts

Heat the oil in a large frying pan or wok, add the ginger and garlic with the tofu and toss together for 1 minute. Add the spring onions and toss again for 1 minute. Mix together the lime juice, chilli sauce and soy sauce, then pour the mixture around the pan so that it heats up before it comes into contact with the food. Add the bean sprouts and toss together for about 1½ minutes. (Don't cook for any longer or the bean sprouts will become soggy.) Serve immediately.

SMOKED TOFU

● Tofu is the name given to soya bean curd in both its original pale white, pressed form and in the smoked version. The pale white variety is virtually flavourless and absorbs other flavours extremely well. So too does the smoked variety but it has more texture as it is firmer and gives a slightly smoky flavour to dishes.

● It's ideal cut into cubes and added to vegetable stews. It has a particular affinity with aubergines, cut to the same size and stir-fried with a little onion, garlic and soy sauce. Very finely shredded, it makes an interesting salad ingredient.

BEANS AND PULSES

● As with most beans, canning seems to be a process that agrees with them. Look, if you can, for a French make, although some of the supermarket own brands are excellent. The beans should be about 1 cm (½ inch) long, pale green in colour and not at all mushy.

● In addition to serving them hot, they make an excellent ingredient for a salad dressed with a mustardy vinaigrette, a very interesting purée with a knob of butter and plenty of black pepper, and an excellent basis for a light soup with some onion, parsley and chicken stock.

Flageolets with Celery and Cream

This is a delicate bean dish, unlike some of the more hearty dishes that beans are usually found in. It's wonderful served with roast lamb or grilled lamb chump chops. I've been serving it for years but until recently always started from scratch with fresh beans. But using a can of flageolet beans, rather than soaking dried beans for hours, makes this a dish that you can put together in an instant. Flageolets, in this case, are the pale green version of haricot beans, not white beans.

time

15 mins

Serves 4

420 g (14½ oz) can flageolet beans
40 g (1½ oz) butter
celery heart, about 5–6 stalks, very thinly sliced
salt and freshly ground black pepper
150 ml (5 fl oz) double cream
1 tablespoon snipped, fresh or frozen chives

Put the beans in a colander, rinse under cold water, then drain. Put in a saucepan with 100 ml (4 fl oz) water, bring slowly to the boil and simmer for 5 minutes.

Melt the butter in a saucepan, add the celery and fry for 2–3 minutes, until beginning to turn golden. Stir in the beans and simmer for 3–4 minutes. Season generously with salt and pepper and add the cream. Return to the boil, stir in the chives and serve immediately.

Flageolet Beans
CRAFTY INGREDIENT

BEANS AND PULSES

Boston Baked Beans Ⓥ

Boston Baked Beans are the ancestor, or forebear if you prefer, of our own canned baked beans, but they have much to recommend them nevertheless. It's particularly easy to make this dish with canned beans (not baked beans) as you don't have to deal with the soaking and long cooking but you're at liberty to make your own flavours. Traditionally, this was eaten on Friday night in Boston, Massachusetts, with a very moist baked bread that also had treacle in it. I think the combination of sweetness is too strong myself, but wholemeal bread eaten with it is still a treat. These beans are also good served with frankfurters or sausages.

time

30 mins

Serves 4

two 420 g (14½ oz) cans white haricot beans
3 tablespoons olive oil or sunflower oil
1 large onion, finely chopped
2 celery sticks, chopped
75 g (3 oz) sun-dried tomatoes, quartered
2 tablespoons tomato purée
1 tablespoon black treacle
salt and freshly ground black pepper

Put the beans in a colander and rinse under cold water.

Heat the oil in a large deep saucepan, add the onion and celery and fry for about 5 minutes, until softened. Add the beans, the sun-dried tomatoes, tomato purée and the treacle. Season generously with salt and pepper, add 500 ml (17 fl oz) water and simmer for 20–25 minutes, stirring 2 or 3 times during cooking.

TOMATO PUREE

● Tomato purée is one of those things we tend to take for granted but until fairly recently it was quite scarce, arriving in tubes about the size of toothpaste tubes and being used as sparingly as that. It's much better in most dishes used generously, as in this one, and makes a great basis for all kinds of tomato sauces and soups, especially when a little extra thickness and sweetness is needed.

● There's a new type now available, sun-dried tomato paste, lighter in colour but more pungent in flavour, which can be used when a slightly smoky flavour is required.

Tomato Purée
CRAFTY INGREDIENT

Onion Bhajis

*In restaurants and, indeed, these days on the fast food counters of some
take-aways, Onion Bhajis come as little balls. In India, they are often made
in a flat pancake shape. This is much easier to achieve and does not require
deep-frying which seems to me to be an enormous bonus. These make a
terrific first course or quite a jolly vegetarian snack. Onion Bhajis are
extraordinarily nutritious because of the gram flour which contains a
substantial amount of protein. Serve these with a dessertspoon or so of
thick, creamy Greek yoghurt and a choice of chutneys.*

time

30 mins

Makes about 12

450g (1 lb) Spanish onions, halved

175 g (6oz) gram flour

1 egg, beaten

½ teaspoon chilli powder

½ teaspoon turmeric

1 tablespoon salt

4 tablespoons cooking oil (not olive oil)

Break the onion slices into individual pieces. Put the gram flour in a
bowl, then stir in the egg, spices, salt, and 300 ml (10 fl oz) water,
whisking continuously for 2–3 minutes, until smooth. Add the onion and
leave to stand for 10 minutes.

Heat the oil in a large frying pan and add half-ladlefuls of the
mixture, making sure you get a mixture of the batter and the onion. It
should spread out to about 5–7 cm (2–3 inches) in the pan and be
irregular in shape. Cook 5–6 at a time for 1½ minutes on each side.
Remove from the pan and keep warm while you cook the remaining
mixture. Serve hot.

GRAM FLOUR

● This golden flour, made from
chick peas, is widely used in
India and South-East Asia for
making various kinds of
pancake as well as being
worked into soups and stews
as a thickener.

● Replacing the onions in this
recipe with some canned
sweetcorn, and using smaller
quantities for each pancake,
makes a wonderful version of
the French Galette au Maïne
so fashionable in good
restaurants.

BEANS AND PULSES

● Technology has created
special bags in which spinach,
harvested young so that it's all
leaf and little stalk, will keep on
the supermarket shelves for
four or five days without any
deterioration. The combination
of growing technologies and
storage methods means that
spinach has become a
transformed product, no
longer requiring long and
tedious picking and trimming.

● It's marvellous on its own,
cooked after washing, in
nothing but a generous knob of
butter on a medium heat, with
a lid on to conserve the juices.
It's also excellent in soups, as a
basis for chicken and eggs in
the Florentine style (see p. 119)
and in its baby leaf form makes
an excellent salad ingredient.

Sag Dhal Ⓥ

*Sag Dhal is an Indian dish combining spinach and lentils, often eaten as one
of the two or three main curries in a vegetarian meal, although it's an
extremely pleasant accompaniment to chicken or any other meat curry as
well. It's a mild dish, very nutritious in its own right and quite pretty to look
at, with its combination of bright green and gold.*

time

30 mins

Serves 4

420 g (14½ oz) can cooked green lentils
2 tablespoons vegetable oil (not olive oil)
250 g (9 oz) onion, finely chopped
1 teaspoon garlic purée
1 teaspoon ginger purée
1 teaspoon chilli powder
1 teaspoon turmeric
1 teaspoon salt
400 g (14 oz) prepared fresh spinach leaves
1 teaspoon garam masala

Put the lentils in a colander and rinse under cold water. Heat the oil in a
saucepan, add the onion, garlic and ginger purée and fry gently until the
onion is softened and translucent. Add the lentils and stir thoroughly.
Add enough water to come 3 cm (1½ inches) above the lentils and stir
in the chilli powder, turmeric and salt. Bring to the boil, then simmer for
15 minutes.

Meanwhile, if necessary, wash the spinach leaves and trim off any
excess stalk. Add to the thick lentil purée, without any additional water,
and cook for another 5 minutes, until the spinach has wilted but is still
green. Stir in the garam masala and leave to stand for 2–3 minutes
before serving.

Spinach
CRAFTY INGREDIENT

BEANS AND PULSES

Oz WINE   The Ideal Wine Glass

Does it really matter what type of glass you drink wine from? Well, yes, it does. Wine sipped from a tiny, thick-lipped tumbler at a picnic may taste fine in the great outdoors but just try it at home at a dinner party!

To maximize pleasure from even the humblest wine, choose a plain, thin glass with a tulip shape and fairly long stem. Make sure that it's big, too – a large glass allows more air to get to the wine which helps to develop the aromas. Now, if you're thinking this is totally unimportant, just try drinking wine with a peg clamped on your nose – you'll hardly taste a thing! Being able to relish the smell of wine is part of the joy of drinking it.

Tips

• As long as the shape is right, there's no sense in spending a fortune on glasses.

• Old-fashioned Champagne saucers may look glamorous but all those bubbles that nature's taken years to produce vanish in a trace! Worse still, it's impossible not to spill at least one mouthful! It's much better to serve fizz in a tall, tapered, bubble-preserving flûte.

• The dishwasher does a good job if you don't pile the glasses in with too many greasy plates. Ideally, wash the glasses separately using hot water only.

• Don't store glasses upside down – they pick up the taint of the shelf.

• The narrowing-necked, tulip shape helps to trap, funnel and magnify all of wine's inviting aromas.

• Fill no more than two-thirds full so that you can easily swirl the contents around without slopping them everywhere! This airs the wine and leaves enough room for you to really stick your nose in for a good sniff!

• The thinner the glass, the finer the taste. Think about it – tea tastes better from bone china than a thick mug – but don't ask me why!

• A long stem keeps the heat of your hand away from the wine.

Most vegetables cook in no time at all. The trouble is the preparation; peeling carrots or onions, washing the sand out of leeks, skinning tomatoes, absorbs time at a terrible rate. The good news, however, is that ready peeled carrots are with us. These prepared vegetables are, of course, more expensive than their unprepared cousins, but in terms of convenience they have no equal. It all began with pre-packed salads which allowed us to buy four or five different colours and textures of lettuce and greens in one bag. Now there are stir-fry packets, with or without their own dressing; cut carrots and swedes, washed baby leeks, topped and tailed beans and mange-tout, washed baby new potatoes and shelled peas. I've even found skinned pickling onions. No don't laugh, these are wonderful. There are few tasks I look forward to less in the kitchen than skinning baby onions, even though I'm not necessarily going to pickle them. (They make a wonderful addition to a rich beef casserole or a sauté of rabbit or chicken.) As you may gather, I'm all in favour of prepared vegetables. Although I don't use them all the time, they do make a terrific difference in terms of effort.

Vegetables can be cooked on their own, turned into vegetable dishes or prepared in interesting and slightly exotic ways to accompany meat, fish or poultry. Some of the techniques I'm using are quite new to us although they may be quite old in the Far East. Stir-frying, for example is something we've become quite used to but it's really quite a recent arrival. It's interesting how little cooking some vegetables actually require. lending themselves perfectly to quick and convenient dishes.

Even if you're just cooking a simple vegetable dish to accompany something else, the addition of some fresh herbs is a terrific idea. A number of flavours go well with each other traditionally, such as thyme with onions and basil with tomatoes, but the range of fresh and quick-frozen herbs now in the shops make it a pleasure to experiment.

Imam Bayildi Ⓥ

The title of this dish always fascinates me as, in Turkish, it literally means 'the imam, (or religious teacher), fainted'. Accounts differ as to whether this was because of the quality or the expense of the dish but this version maintains the quality and certainly wouldn't make him faint through the expense.

time

30 mins

Serves 4

4 tablespoons olive oil

450 g (1 lb) aubergines, cut lengthways into 1 cm (½ inch) thick
slices

1 garlic clove, finely chopped, or 1 teaspoon garlic purée

250 g (9 oz) onions, finely chopped

400 g (14½ oz) can chopped Italian tomatoes with pizza herbs

pinch of ground cinnamon

pinch of ground allspice

salt and freshly ground black pepper

pinch of sugar, if necessary

chopped fresh parsley, to garnish

4 lemon wedges, to serve

Pre-heat the oven to 200°C/400°F/Gas 6.

Heat 2 tablespoons of olive oil in a frying pan, add the aubergine slices and fry gently for 2–3 minutes on each side, until light golden.

Meanwhile, heat the remaining oil in a saucepan. Add the garlic and onions and fry gently, stirring occasionally for about 5 minutes, until softened. Stir in the chopped tomatoes and 100 ml (4 fl oz) water, bring to the boil and simmer for 5 minutes. Add the cinnamon and allspice and season generously with salt and pepper. Taste and add the sugar, if necessary, to bring out the full flavour of the tomatoes.

Spread a thin layer of the tomato sauce in an ovenproof dish. Add a layer of aubergine and then a generous layer of the tomatoes, the remaining aubergine and finally the tomatoes.

Bake in the oven for 15–20 minutes, until bubbling. Garnish with plenty of chopped parsley and serve with the lemon wedges to squeeze over.

HERBED CANNED TOMATOES

● In addition to being canned in their own juice and chopped to save us the trouble of having to do so, Italian tomatoes are also now being flavoured with herbs.

● They come in two or three varieties, basil, pizza herbs and oregano, and I find them very useful for making all kinds of simmered and baked dishes that abound in the Mediterranean, whether in Italy, Turkey, Lebanon or Spain.

● They can also be used in the way some of them were intended, as a ready flavoured pizza topping, but I'd add a few more herbs of my own to make the flavour more intense.

VEGETABLES

88

● Like so many nuts, hazelnuts are delicious to eat but tedious to prepare if you have to start with the nuts in their shells. They now come shelled in a variety of styles in our supermarkets. The cheapest, and the variety for this dish, is already chopped but you can also get them whole or halved, natural or toasted

● They are excellent in muesli, a key ingredient in a number of cakes and, sprinkled with a little salt, pretty good as a snack in their own right, especially the toasted ones.

Hazelnut and Courgette Gratin

I like gratins. They're very simple to make, they cook quickly and, in my experience, everyone loves them. Originally, the word 'gratin' meant something topped with breadcrumbs and you can, indeed, still make gratins in exactly that way. But I'm fond of experimenting with the toppings as well as the main ingredients and find that this combination of vegetables and nuts is particularly good.

time

30 mins

Serves 4

25 g (1 oz) butter
1 tablespoon olive or sunflower oil
450 g (1 lb) courgettes, cut into 1 cm (½ inch) thick slices
salt and freshly ground black pepper
2 eggs, beaten
150 ml (5 fl oz) single cream
50 g (2 oz) chopped hazelnuts
50 g (2 oz) freshly grated Parmesan or Pecorino cheese

Pre-heat the oven to 180°C/350°F/Gas 5.

Melt the butter and oil in a frying pan, add the courgette slices and fry gently for 4–5 minutes until golden brown. Remove from the pan and put in a gratin dish. Season generously with salt and pepper. Beat together the eggs and cream and pour over the dish. Mix the hazelnuts with the cheese and sprinkle over the top.

Bake in the oven for about 25 minutes, until the eggs and cream have just set around the courgettes and the topping is a light golden brown.

VEGETABLES

Hazelnuts
CRAFTY INGREDIENT

Baked Duchesse Tomatoes (V)

This recipe is an adaptation of a dish I first had at the house of some friends close to Bordeaux in the South-West of France. It uses the huge Marmande tomatoes which are so common in France throughout the summer, full of flavour and delightfully irregular in shape. The nearest equivalent we get here are beefsteak tomatoes, similar in size but I'm afraid often lacking the flavour, or indeed the shape. They do, however, still make a delicious dish using the tomato shells as a casing for a herb and cheese stuffing. This was originally served with grilled duck breasts but goes equally well with most grilled meats and makes a perfectly splendid first course.

time

20 mins

Serves 4

RICOTTA

2 large beefsteak tomatoes

175 g (6 oz) ricotta cheese

2 teaspoons snipped fresh or frozen chives

salt and freshly ground black pepper

2 slices white bread

I garlic clove, finely chopped

1–2 tablespoons olive oil (optional)

Pre-heat the grill. Cut the tomatoes in half widthways and, using a very sharp knife and a teaspoon, scoop out as much of the insides as you can, leaving a firm shell. Discard the juices and finely chop the flesh. Put in a bowl and stir in the ricotta cheese and chives and season generously with salt and pepper. Use the mixture to fill the tomato shells.

Put the bread in a food processor and blend into breadcrumbs. Add the chopped garlic and mix together. Top the filled tomatoes with a layer of breadcrumbs and sprinkle them with olive oil, if you wish.

Place under the grill at a distance of 7.5–10 cm (3–4 inches) from the heat, and cook for about 15 minutes, until the tomatoes are hot and the breadcrumbs dark brown but not burnt. Transfer to warmed serving plates.

RICOTTA

● Ricotta is made from the whey of milk from which the cream has been removed. It's therefore low in fat and very mild. It's often incorporated in pastries, in the pastry itself as an alternative to butter, as part of a filling, and when making Italian cheesecakes.

● It's also good in salads, particularly with herbs or nuts, and as part of the filling for many Italian stuffed pastas.

VEGETABLES

Crafty Dauphinoise Potatoes

Pommes Dauphinoise is one of the great dishes of France – garlicky layers of potato baked to a golden crust in cream and butter. It does, however, normally take about 1½ hours in the oven and for some years I attempted to develop alternatives that didn't take quite so long. Two or three sources led me in this direction and, although I must admit that it's not the same as the ultimate slow-baked-to-perfection version, it's still quite delicious. It's particularly good with chops, liver and other meats that need a creamy vegetable to go with them.

time

30 mins

Serves 4

50 g (2 oz) butter
450 g (1 lb) potatoes
600 ml (1 pint) breakfast or gold top milk
1 teaspoon garlic salt
freshly ground black pepper

Use 25 g (1 oz) of the butter to grease a gratin dish. Peel the potatoes and cut them into 5 mm (¼ inch) thick slices. Put them in a saucepan, add the milk, bring slowly to the boil, and simmer for 8–10 minutes.

Pre-heat the grill. Using a slotted spoon, remove the potatoes from the milk and layer them in the prepared dish, sprinkling each layer with the garlic salt and pepper. Pour enough of the milk into the dish to come just below the top layer of the potatoes. Dot the potatoes with the remaining butter.

Place under the grill, about 8 cm (3 inches) away from the heat, and cook for about 10 minutes, until the top is browned and bubbling.

BREAKFAST MILK

● Breakfast milk is the modern marketing name for what we used to call Channel Island milk, an extremely rich, full-cream milk, unfortunately far from the fashionable semi-skimmed and skimmed milk which we are encouraged to use today. It does, however, have a wonderful texture and great flavour and is superb if you can afford the fat content (about 6 per cent) on breakfast cereals.

● It's excellent for certain kinds of cooking for which the low-fat varieties are not suitable. Custards are one example, good white sauce is another and milk puddings, such as rice or bread and butter, really cry out for its extra richness.

● I wouldn't use it in tea although it is helpful in coffee, but if you fancy a glass of ice cold milk nothing beats this.

● It's usually homogenized, which means that the cream has been whisked so it won't separate.

VEGETABLES

Stir-fried Leeks with Celery and Light Soy Sauce

● Soy sauce comes in a number of varieties and thicknesses. Light soy sauce, sometimes called superior soy sauce, the kind that Japanese soy sauce or shoyu is made from, is the lightest and most delicate of all. It increases the flavour of foods without significantly altering their taste so it's excellent with light coloured meats such as chicken, whether in a stir-fry or a marinade.

● It's best for fish, both shellfish and whole fish. In small quantities, like half a teaspoon, it adds an unexpected fillip to salad dressings, and is good in the same sort of quantities when added to individual bowls of soup, particularly those lacking any meat base or stock.

For many years, leeks were regarded as very much a second-class vegetable, the sort of thing you would put into soups, but recently their flavour and value has become more apparent. This dish uses the Chinese technique of stir-frying and some Chinese flavours to go with it, although it should not be thought of as a Chinese dish but as a quick and easy way of cooking one of our best winter vegetables. It goes well with grilled steaks and fish, to balance the flavours and textures. It also makes a perfectly good vegetarian dish in it own right, particularly eaten with a brown rice pilau and perhaps the Baked Duchesse Tomatoes *on page 90.*

time
15 mins

Serves 4

450 g (1 lb) leeks
2 tablespoons olive oil
1 teaspoon chopped ginger or ginger purée
salt and freshly ground pepper
1 celery head, cut into 1 cm (½ inch) thick slices
3 tablespoons light soy sauce

Trim the tops and bottoms of the leeks and cut in half lengthways. Wash them carefully in plenty of cold water, then drain. Slice the leeks widthways into 4 pieces then cut those widthways into 1 cm (½ inch) slices. Heat the oil in a large frying pan or wok, add the leeks and toss and turn with a spatula for about 2 minutes. Add the ginger and season generously with salt and pepper. Add the celery and continue to stir-fry over a medium heat for another 4–5 minutes, until softened but not soggy. Raise the heat to high and pour the soy sauce around the edges of the pan so it runs down into the vegetables. Toss together lightly and quickly, then serve at once.

VEGETABLES

Storing, Decanting and Chilling

STORING WINE

Any wine that you're not going to open within a few weeks of purchase is worth storing properly – yes, even those multi-saver bottles! After all, wine is a living thing and even the most resilient reacts badly to the wrong environment. Just a little care will go a long way to increasing the chance of squeezing every single drop of enjoyment from every bottle.

Temperature

The exact degree isn't as important as maintaining a steady ambient temperature. Frequent fluctuations cause havoc to wine's make-up, so don't fall into the tempting trap of keeping wine in the garage!

Choose the coolest room in the house and store wine in a cupboard, wardrobe or drawers. Any form of insulation helps such as cardboard, wood, polystyrene and even kitchen foil.

The kitchen tends to be a super-conductor of heat so avoid long-term storage here. Having said that, keep a bottle of red handy so there's always one ready at room temperature.

Bottle Position

Bottles really do need to lie on their sides – the cork then stays damp and keeps out the air.

DECANTING

Any wine, even whites, can be decanted but few actually need to be. Reds which have thrown a sediment, along with some styles of Port, are the exception – unless you're really into drinking mouthfuls of sandy sludge!

All you need is a torch and a steady hand. The task is made much easier if you allow the deposit to settle by standing the bottle upright for a few days.

- Don't decant until the last moment – a couple of hours in advance at the most.
- Remove the cork, keeping the bottle vertical.
- Aim the beam of the torch upwards under the bottle's neck.
- Carefully pour the wine in one smooth, continuous movement until you see the arrowhead of sediment reach the neck.
- Don't throw the sediment away – add it to the cooking pot!

CHILLING...AND WARMING

There's no doubt about it, white wines do taste better cold and reds are easier to drink at the right degree of warmth. However, how cold is cold and how warm is warm and what do you do when your whites are too warm and your reds are too cold?

- For whites and rosés, an hour in the fridge door is about right, although purists insist on 7-10°C (45-50°F). Sauvignon Blanc doesn't mind an extra bit of chilling.
- Sweet and sparkling wines need to be slightly cooler (4.5-7°C/40-45°F). A couple of hours in the fridge is perfect.
- Over-chilling masks the more subtle aromas and flavours of the wine.
- To quickly chill wine, plunge into ice and water for 15 minutes. Twenty minutes in the freezer is equally effective and, contrary to popular belief, it doesn't harm wine.
- Red wines suffer from our centrally-heated, hothouse culture. Room temperature is not what it was! Aim for a cooler 15°C (60°F).
- Many light reds, such as Beaujolais, are really appealing lightly-chilled.
- Warming red wines commands care because the process is irreversible. Immerse in tepid water or go for the DIY approach – cradle the glass in warm hands.

Caraway Seeds
CRAFTY INGREDIENT

Stir-tossed Caraway Cabbage Ⓥ

Very few cooks can lay claim to original cooking techniques. This may be the closest I've ever come as I've adapted the concept of high-speed cooking for vegetables from the Chinese but using essentially European ingredients, equipment and flavours. This is the most delicious way I know of eating cabbage and it converts even the hardened greens-haters. The flavour and colour are just astonishing and quite a revelation when it comes to cabbage. I've suggested caraway seeds here which make a wonderful accompaniment but it can be cooked just as it is and works equally well as a technique with spring greens and quartered sprouts. Serve the cabbage as a vegetable dish with meat and potatoes or as one of two or three vegetable dishes cooked in their own right and eaten as a vegetarian meal.

time

5 mins

Serves 4

750 g (1½ lb) green, hearty cabbage
25 g (1 oz) butter
1 teaspoon caraway seeds
salt and freshly ground black pepper

Trim the cabbage and slice it widthways into 5 mm (¼ inch) strips. When you get to the heart, cut it in half, then slice it into 5 mm (¼ inch) strips. Put the butter and 150 ml (5 fl oz) water into a large saucepan, with a close-fitting lid, and bring it to the boil. Add the caraway seeds and then the cabbage. Put the lid on and cook for 1 minute. Shake the pan vigorously while holding the lid down tightly. Remove the lid, season generously with salt and pepper, then shake again and cook for another minute. (Do not be tempted to cook it for longer.) Serve hot, with the buttery juices poured over the cabbage.

CARAWAY SEEDS

● These small, highly flavoured seeds are much used in Europe to flavour cabbage and cabbage-based dishes such as Sauerkraut.
● They are used for flavouring cooked meat and make a splendid addition, in small quantities, to a pot roast or beef stew.
● Try them in baking, and a few sprinkled on top of home-made biscuits before they go into the oven or on to a seed cake, make a wonderful fragrant addition.

VEGETABLES

96

● These are batons of carrot
about the size of your little
finger, ready peeled and
prepared. In fact they come
from large, long, thin carrots
grown specially for the
purpose. They're quite
delicious.
● One of the suggestions of
the producers is that they
make a marvellous lunch box
addition and a particularly
healthy one for young children.
● They are excellent for
crudités, for dips, to add to
beef or chicken stew and split
or shredded in salads.
● They have the added virtue
of being able to be kept in the
bottom of the fridge for 2–3
days without any
deterioration.

Carrots with Star Anise

*The flavours of aniseed and carrots make a wonderful combination. Star
anise is a bright, shiny seed contained in a seed pod with about five or six of
them forming a star shape. It comes from South-East Asia and, while it's
pungent, it has a restrained flavour, very good with foods that are not
necessarily a South-East Asian meal. The technique used is that of Carrots
Vichy, the style of cooking carrots that's supposed to be the best in France.
You can, if you like, leave out the star anise and still get very good carrots
although you'll be missing quite an extraordinary flavour.*

time

20 mins

Serves 4

350 g (12 oz) prepared carrot batons
½ teaspoon salt
3 star anise
25 g(1 oz) butter
½ teaspoon sugar

Put all the ingredients in a saucepan into which they all fit to a depth of
5–7.5cm (2–3 inches). Add cold water to 1 cm (½) inch below the level
of the top of the carrots. Bring slowly to the boil, cover, then simmer for
5 minutes. Uncover and boil for 8–9 minutes, until most of the liquid has
evaporated and the carrots are glazed.

Carrot Batons
CRAFTY INGREDIENT

MAIN
MEALS

FISH

One of the most encouraging things in the recent development of food shopping, has been the emphasis placed on fish. There are fish of all sorts. Companies with formidable reputations for running fish and chip shops have even begun to produce frozen versions of their take-away meals to be bought from the supermarket freezer cabinet. In addition, a whole range of new, fresh and prepared fish has emerged. Salmon now comes in three or four different pre-packed cuts and trout has followed it, with whole and headless fish and fillets. On the seafood front, both raw and prepared prawns, North Atlantic and Tropical Tiger, are regularly available, as are ready prepared mussels and some very interesting mixtures of shellfish and seafood designed to be used in dishes such as seafood salads. Be careful to look for mixes that haven't got any vinegar in them.

In addition there are a number of new varieties of fish, usually in the form of fillets, such as bream. These are emerging, I suspect, because of the shortage of our more traditional fish, such as haddock and cod, from the North Sea. They are, however, quite delicious and very well worth cooking in both modern and traditional methods. There are also a number of very good pickled herrings in jars or tubs that make a delicious hors d'oeuvre or addition to a scrambled egg supper. As well as salmon, there are all kinds of smoked fish, including trout and halibut, and some very interestingly flavoured smoked mackerel, which comes now in peppered and garlic versions as well as natural. And don't forget that fish cans wonderfully: everything from small anchovy fillets, which go so well on salads or pizzas, through to the substantial tuna, now available in brine as well as oil, a crucial ingredient in a number of dishes including the fabulous *Salade Niçoise*. Canned, frozen or fresh, there's no question that the range of fish now available is marvellous, and all fish has one other advantage: it cooks quickly, so it's always a crafty option.

Thai Curry Paste

CRAFTY INGREDIENT

THAI CURRY PASTE

● Thai curry paste is a particularly useful ready-made ingredient because the number of flavours and spices that go into it are quite considerable and, even now, one or two of them are difficult to obtain in this country. The principal flavours are galangal, a ginger-like root, and chillies, with lemon grass and coriander.

● It can be used in a variety of marinades but it's primary use is in a curry made in a similar manner to that described here. The same recipe is frequently used for chicken and, even sometimes beef, in Thailand.

Thai Prawn Curry

Thai food has become increasingly popular in recent years and the originally quite unusual ingredients required are suddenly widely available. It's a clean-tasting cuisine, with the sharpness of citrus, usually coming from limes, and some quite fiery but subtle flavours from the curry ingredients. These days it's possible to buy different coloured curry pastes to make the curries; the red is the mildest and the green is the strongest. This recipe is a dish to eat with rice, or it can be part of a meal with a wider combination of Thai dishes. This would usually include some soup, a spicy salad and a stir-fry of chicken or meat and vegetables, as well as the prawn curry and rice.

time

15 mins

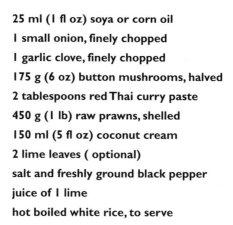

Serves 4

25 ml (I fl oz) soya or corn oil
I small onion, finely chopped
I garlic clove, finely chopped
175 g (6 oz) button mushrooms, halved
2 tablespoons red Thai curry paste
450 g (I lb) raw prawns, shelled
150 ml (5 fl oz) coconut cream
2 lime leaves (optional)
salt and freshly ground black pepper
juice of I lime
hot boiled white rice, to serve

Heat the oil in a frying pan and gently fry the onion and garlic for 2–3 minutes, until translucent but not brown. Put the button mushrooms in a colander and run under very hot water for 1–2 minutes until completely washed and clean.

Add the red Thai curry paste to the onion and cook gently for a further minute. Add the prawns and turn to coat them thoroughly with the mixture. Stir in the coconut cream and the lime leaves, if using, season with salt and pepper and bring to the boil. Simmer for not more than 1–2 minutes or the prawns will become rubbery. When the mixture is well mixed, remove from the heat, add the lime juice and serve with rice.

FISH

101

Prawn Kebabs with Instant Satay Sauce

These days you can buy already skewered raw tiger prawns, about six or so on a skewer, from many fish counters, and if you can find them these are ideal. If not, buy your own tiger prawns and wooden bamboo skewers and make your own. The sauce, by the way, goes equally well with any kebab made with any meaty fish. Cut the fish into 2 cm (¾ inch) chunks and thread them on a skewer. This is best served with rice and a salad containing bean sprouts.

time

25 mins

Serves 4

> **350 g (12 oz) tiger prawns, shelled, or 8 pre-prepared**
> **prawn skewers**
> **4 tablespoons soy sauce**
> **1 teaspoon caster sugar**
> **1 tablespoon rice vinegar or cider vinegar**
> **1 tablespoon sunflower or corn oil**
> **4 tablespoons crunchy peanut butter**

Pre-heat the grill and line the grill pan with foil.

Thread the prawns equally on to 8 bamboo skewers, keeping the prawns close together and finishing about 2 cm (¾ inch) from the sharp tip. Put in a large, shallow dish. Mix together the soy sauce, sugar and vinegar, pour over the prawns and leave to marinate for 15 minutes.

Place the skewers in the grill pan, reserving the marinate. Brush the prawns lightly with the oil and grill for not more than 2–3 minutes on each side until tender. (If cooked longer they will become rubbery.)

Meanwhile, in a saucepan, mix together the reserved marinade, the peanut butter and 150 ml (5 fl oz) water. Bring to the boil, stirring vigorously, until the mixture is well mixed and smooth.

Drizzle some of the sauce over the prawn skewers and serve the rest in a bowl or sauce boat.

PEANUT BUTTER

● Although a familiar ingredient, this now comes in a wide variety of forms. Look for one that's made without added sugar or any emulsifiers or added flavours.

● Smooth or crunchy doesn't make a great difference except when making a satay sauce, which was traditionally made from whole peanuts which were ground.

● Peanut butter has the capacity, rather like flour or tomato purée, to make a smooth and velvety sauce when it's mixed with water and heated.

● This satay sauce recipe can be used for other grilled meats and fish.

● It's very good spread on toast if you have any left over.

Peanut Butter
CRAFTY INGREDIENT

Cod in Old-fashioned Parsley Sauce

This is one of those dishes that the hideous memories from school have blotted out from our minds. This is not right because, properly made, cod with an old-fashioned, thick, green, parsley sauce has wonderful flavours and textures to it. In my opinion, this dish goes best with a large heap of well-mashed creamy potatoes.

time

25 mins

Serves 4

750 g (1½ lb) cod fillet, divided into 4 pieces
40 g (1½ oz) cornflour
40 g (1½ oz) butter, cubed
500 ml (17 fl oz) full-cream milk
pinch of ground nutmeg
50 g (2 oz) chopped frozen parsley
salt and freshly ground black pepper
hot mashed potato, to serve

Put the cod in a colander, sprinkle with 1 tablespoon salt and leave for 15 minutes, before rinsing the salt off thoroughly. (This draws some of the moisture out of the fish and makes it firmer and more succulent to eat.) Place the colander over a saucepan of boiling water, not letting the colander touch the water. Cover with a lid and steam for 7–10 minutes, depending on the thickness of the fish. It should be cooked right the way through and be opaque but not in any sense dried out.

Meanwhile, in a pan, whisk the cornflour and butter into the milk and heat gently, whisking all the time until the mixture comes to the boil and is very thick and smooth. Add the nutmeg and a little salt and pepper. Stir in the parsley.

Carefully remove the cod from the colander and arrange on individual plates. Pour over 1–2 spoonfuls of parsley sauce and serve the rest in a jug to add to both the fish and the mashed potato.

FROZEN PARSLEY

● This comes in two forms, free-flowing and in little egg-shaped parcels. Either is suitable for this dish and it's amazing how unaffected by freezing parsley is.

● If you have the patience, you can even make your own ice cubes of frozen parsley, which is effectively what the little egg-shaped parcels are.

● Freezing herbs keeps their flavour and colour much more vividly than any other methods of preserving them.

● The free-flowing frozen parsley is good for using in all sorts of other dishes where a good sprinkling of parsley is needed.

FISH

Baked Trout Fillets with Spiced Yoghurt

This is a simple way of cooking fish using the tandoori method, much favoured in Northern India. We forget that India is surrounded by coastline and has many rivers; this means that fish, which is almost as popular as meat in the subcontinent. Indeed, in some places it's even more popular, and when you taste this simple but succulent way of cooking trout you'll realize why.

time

25 mins

TROUT FILLETS

● Farmed trout has become so widely available now that we tend to rather take it for granted but it's not very long ago that trout was a huge luxury. Farmed trout is now one of the most delicious and economical ingredients around.

● It comes not only as whole fish but also in fillets, which make it even easier to eat, especially for those people for whom bones are anathema.

● As well as being cooked in this spicy way, it's particularly nice just floured and fried in a little oil and butter in the old-fashioned meunière style.

Serves 4

4 large or 8 small trout fillets

FOR THE MARINADE:
225 ml (8 fl oz) natural Greek yoghurt
1 tablespoon tandoori tikka paste
juice of 1 lemon
½ onion, very finely sliced
hot rice or naan bread, to serve

Pre-heat the oven to 220°C/425°F/Gas 7.

Place the trout fillets in a non-metallic dish in a single layer. In a separate bowl, mix together the yoghurt, tandoori paste (disregarding any instructions on the jar for using more as this is meant to be a mild-tasting dish), the lemon juice and the onion. Pour over the trout to thoroughly coat it and leave to marinate for 5 minutes.

Cook in the oven for 10–15 minutes, depending on the size of the fillets, until tender and browning on the edges but not in any way dry. Serve with rice or hot naan bread and salad.

Trout
CRAFTY INGREDIENT

Truffle Oil
CRAFTY INGREDIENT

Salmon Steaks Grilled with Truffle Oil

Truffles are those incredibly expensive underground mushrooms which appear principally in Italy and France and are used to flavour food. By far the easiest, and indeed the most economical way of obtaining their flavour is by using oil, usually olive oil, which has been soaked and impregnated with the truffle essence. It produces a rich flavour, not overwhelming, which goes particularly well with fish. Salmon steaks, of course, are easily obtained these days.

time

25 mins

Serves 4

4 salmon steaks
juice of 1 lemon
1 tablespoon truffle oil
450 g (1 lb) courgettes
50 ml (2 fl oz) sunflower oil
1 garlic clove, finely chopped

Pre-heat the grill and line the grill pan with foil.

Put the salmon steaks in a china or glass dish into which they just fit and squeeze over half the lemon juice. Turn them so that there is lemon juice on both sides. Drizzle the truffle oil over each salmon steak, and leave to marinate for about 10 minutes.

Place the salmon steaks in the grill pan and grill them for 3–4 minutes on each side, until tender, but still moist in the centre.

Meanwhile, top and tail the courgettes and cut in half lengthways. Using a teaspoon, scoop out the soft seeds, then, using a mandolin or grater, grate the courgettes lengthways into long thin strips like spaghetti. Alternatively, using a sharp knife, cut the courgettes lengthways into thin strips but you don't get such fine pieces. In a medium frying pan, heat the oil and fry the garlic for 1 minute, then add the courgette spaghetti and fry for 3–4 minutes.

Put the salmon steaks on to warmed plates, arrange the courgettes around them, squeeze over the remaining lemon juice and serve hot.

FISH

TRUFFLE OIL

● Truffle oil comes in small and quite expensive bottles. They're usually rather attractive and the labelling and sealing can be quite elaborate but the key thing to look for is the country of origin. If they're French or Italian they have a much stronger likelihood of containing the best essence of truffle.

● The oil itself can be kept in a dark cupboard for up to a year and can be used to flavour salad dressings, in marinades for other grills, particularly red meats, and with eggs, for frying an omelette or an Italian *Frittata* (see p. 69) made with mushrooms.

Wine with Fish

There's an astonishing number of different fish around. The White Fish Authority lists over 52 edible species in home waters alone and this total doesn't include shell or freshwater fish! With such a cornucopia of flavours, it stands to reason that the wine should be more exciting than just plain dry white!

The rule that only whites will do is patently silly when a red can be far better with some fish. Michael's *Salmon Steaks Grilled with Truffle Oil* for example, tastes terrific with a light Pinot Noir or top quality Beaujolais. Although a gentle white is usually best with bream and trout, Michael's recipes lend themselves to soft, pretty pink rosés from southern France or Spain.

Fish with rich sauces clamours for solid, weighty, buttery Chardonnay guzzlers (traditional Côte d'Or white Burgundies or oak-aged, Australian styles) or a Sauvignon Blanc with crunchy acidity (Bordeaux Blanc or white Graves).

Delicate seafood dishes need subtle, mouth-watering, bone-dry styles, which is why Muscadet is such a classic. However, the Spanish have the brightest idea; they chill dry Sherry, serve it in massive glasses and swill it down with their seafood. It's a cracking combination!

Spicy prawn recipes need either a spicy wine to match — an oily, lychee-and-rosewater touched Alsace Gewürztraminer is ideal — or a slightly sweeter wine. Try a German Morio Muskat or Piesporter.

Finally, what to serve with the fishy treat of lobster? Push the boat out (sorry!) and indulge in a top-notch Chablis or Sancerre, the priciest you can afford. As for the salty tang of oysters, wash down with Champagne…mmm, a lip-smacking marriage made in heaven!

Tips

● Very oily fish, are wine killers. Serve Sherry instead.

● Fish served plain and simple needs simple wines. Easy-drinking, dryish, cool climate, European wines are the best all-rounders and won't cost the earth.

● You can save the more expensive wines to serve with recipes with rich sauces. Incidentally, the sauce is the most important element of any wine-and-fish-matching exercise, so think of the sauce first and the fish second.

● Battered fish can stand a weightier, more flavoursome wine. Unoaked New World Chardonnays — and even light rosés — work well. A word of warning, however! If it's fish and chips from the local chippy, go easy on the vinegar (or better still, avoid it altogether) if you want any hope of enjoying the wine!

Bream Fillets with Peperonata

Sea bream is a fish you tend to find at the fishmonger's rather than on supermarket shelves. It's a round fish, red-skinned, with quite meaty fillets and a delicious flavour. One of the reasons it's not used more often is that the skin is covered in very substantial scales which need removing. Make sure your fishmonger does it for you. This recipe makes use of one of the many styles of ready made pasta sauces available, which go particularly well with the meaty and succulent bream fillets. The fennel adds a nice, slightly aniseed note, which lifts the sauce and makes it specially suited to the flavours of fish.

time

25 mins

Serves 4

4 bream fillets, each weighing about 100g (4 oz)
25–50 g/(1–2 oz) plain flour
50 ml (2 fl oz) sunflower oil
1 fennel head, cut into 5mm (¼ inch) slices
350 g (12 oz) jar peperonata pasta sauce
juice of 1 lemon
salt and freshly ground black pepper
rice or sauté potatoes, to serve

Coat the bream fillets in flour, shaking off any excess flour from each fillet. In a large frying pan, heat the oil and fry the fennel for 4–5 minutes, until pale golden. Push the fennel to one side of the pan.

Add the bream fillets, cut surface down, and fry for 3–4 minutes then turn and cook for a further 3–4 minutes, until tender. Add the peperonata sauce, then stir into the fennel. Bring to the boil and simmer for 2–3 minutes. Stir in the lemon juice and season with salt and pepper. Serve with rice or sauté potatoes.

PEPERONATA PASTA SAUCE

● Peperonata pasta sauce is made with red and green peppers. The best have strips or chunks of peppers in them and, as most of them come in transparent jars, it's worth having a careful look at them and choosing one with substantial pieces in, as these will probably have the best flavour and texture.

● The sauce can be used to casserole other fish and chicken, or even on pasta, as it was originally designed.

FISH

Peperonata
CRAFTY INGREDIENT

Chicken has become our favourite meat. It surpassed beef even before the BSE crisis gave it an extra impetus. It's not really surprising, because it's one of the most versatile meats and it comes in many different forms. Frozen chicken is widely available and, if thawed properly, it is remarkably good value and reasonable in flavour. Chilled is the most commonly available variety and the choice is enormous. There are all sizes, from tiny poussin, which will just feed two, to large family-sized birds that will feed six to eight. They also come in a variety of rearing styles: including the standard battery-style chicken; corn-fed, often bright yellow in colour and raised on an exclusively vegetarian diet; and free-range, which get a lot more fresh air and exercise with flavour and texture to prove it. Last but not least, although they're not always readily available in supermarkets, are organic or farmyard birds, raised with an even more liberal lifestyle but with a price tag to match.

In addition, most poultry (not only chicken but also turkey and duck) comes in portions such as breasts, skinless thighs, fillets, leg portions, stir-fry strips and mince which are all worth trying. Not least, these portions allow you to buy as much as you need for a specific meal without having leftovers to worry about or a surplus to use in some other meal. If you do buy a whole chicken though and don't use it all, remember that the bones and carcass, even in this modern day, make wonderful stock. I also often save the skin, cut it into small pieces and fry it in a hot, dry pan until the fat runs out. This leaves lovely, crackly pieces of skin that the French call *grissons*, which are terrific sprinkled over a green salad dressed in olive oil and red wine vinegar.

POULTRY

Quick Chicken Karai

A karai is a wok from the north of India, usually smaller than Chinese ones. They're used to produce the quick-fried curries that sometimes, in a rather denigrated version, are known in Britain as baltis, but a good karai doesn't have the surplus liquid that those dishes seem to have. Whilst I am suggesting chicken for this dish, it would go equally well with finely sliced lamb or beef, although you need to adjust the type of masala paste you use. Chutneys and poppadoms make good accompaniments.

time

25 mins

Serves 4

1 tablespoon vegetable oil

25 g (1 oz) butter

450 g (1 lb) boneless chicken thighs, quartered

2 tablespoons chicken masala paste

1 large Spanish onion, diced

1 red pepper, seeded and cut into 2.5 cm (1 inch) cubes

1 green pepper, seeded and cut into 2.5 cm (1 inch) cubes

175 g (6 oz) cherry tomatoes, halved

salt and freshly ground black pepper

juice of 1 lemon

2 teaspoons brown sugar

hot cooked rice, to serve

Heat the oil and butter in a karai or wok and gently fry the chicken for about 5 minutes, until brown. Stir in the masala paste and fry for a further 5 minutes. Add the onion, peppers, tomatoes and 125 ml (4 fl oz) water. Cook for a further 10–12 minutes, until the chicken is tender and the vegetables are cooked but not wilted. Season with salt and pepper and add the lemon juice and brown sugar. Stir thoroughly and leave to stand for 5 minutes before serving with rice.

MASALA PASTE

● Masala, tikka and curry pastes now come in many varieties. The best advice is to avoid those that are too brightly coloured and to make sure it's paste you're selecting and not a ready made sauce.

● Many of these pastes are designated for their appropriate meats, such as chicken, beef, prawn or fish. It's best to choose the correct one even though the only difference will be the balance of the spices.

● I would advise you to always use less than is recommended. I find a tablespoon or two is as much as I would want as a flavouring for the ingredients for four people.

● They are an excellent alternative to curry powder in many Indian recipes and a teaspoon in Parsnip Soup is delicious.

Masala Paste
CRAFTY INGREDIENT

Prawn Stuffed Chicken Pockets

This recipe is suitable for quite a smart dinner party and is inspired by both Chinese and, unlikely though it may seem, Australian originals. In fact, Australian food, under the influence of South-East Asia, has become one of the most interesting cuisines in the world. This recipe combines two delicate flavours that really complement each other. I like to serve it with a wild and basmati rice pilau or new potatoes and a green vegetable such as string beans or broccoli.

time

25 mins

Serves 4

100 g (4 oz) raw prawns, shelled
1 teaspoon ginger purée
1 egg white
juice of 1 lemon
4 boneless chicken breasts
25 ml (1 fl oz) vegetable oil
25 g (1 oz) butter
2 tablespoons soy sauce

Put the prawns, ginger, egg white and half of the lemon juice in a food processor and blend until smooth. (You can leave a little texture in it but it should be thoroughly mixed together.)

Using a sharp knife, cut the chicken breasts lengthways to make a pocket in each. Spread the prawn mixture inside each of the chicken breasts. Then fasten the pockets with either a cocktail stick or bamboo skewer threaded like very coarse stitching.

Heat the oil and butter in a frying pan, add the chicken breasts and fry for 5 minutes on each side. Cover and leave to cook over a low heat for a further 5–10 minutes, until cooked through. (The prawn mixture will have become firm during cooking.) Remove the chicken from the pan and keep warm. Pour in the pan with the soy sauce and the remaining lemon juice. Pour the sauce over the chicken breasts and serve hot.

BONELESS AND SKINLESS CHICKEN BREASTS

● Boneless and skinless chicken breasts are the most expensive way to buy chicken but, as with so many of the portioned chicken pieces that you can buy, everything from mince to boned thighs, it's quite a practical way to buy the meat if you have a specific recipe in mind.
● It's worth looking for the free-range breasts for flavour.
● Use for other luxury chicken dishes like chicken in tarragon or cut in chunks for special kebabs.

POULTRY

Marinated Chicken and Fig Kebabs

BOTTLED
MARINADES

● In my experience, the best bottle marinades are those that aren't thick like ketchup but are thin and have spices in them which seem to make them able to penetrate the meat more and provide more flavour.

● The ones with the West Indian background, which are often called by the name of the Island of Barbados, seem to have the most exciting spices and combinations of flavours.

● They can be used with a variety of meats and ingredients regardless of the instructions on the bottle.

There's no traditional origin for this dish yet it's a happy combination that I discovered after various experiments. If you don't like sweet and sour flavours together, you probably won't like this, but if you do, it's a real winner. Fresh figs are surprisingly often available in the summer in Britain. Most people don't know what to do with them and are even afraid of just eating them as a fruit. This is a lovely way of using them where their texture and slightly spiced sweetness go brilliantly with the chicken and the marinade. You can barbecue this dish or cook it on the grill in your kitchen. I find that the flour tortillas that are available everywhere now go particularly well with this.

time

30 mins

Serves 4

4 boneless chicken breasts, skinned and each cut into
   6 equal pieces
6 tablespoons bottled Barbados-style chicken marinade
8 bay leaves
4 large black or green figs, quartered

Pre-heat the grill or a barbecue. Marinate the chicken pieces in the Barbados-style marinade for 15 minutes.

Using 4 large, flat-sided metal skewers, thread a bay leaf on to each skewer, then a piece of chicken, a fig and repeat with the chicken and figs until there are 6 chicken pieces and 4 fig pieces on each skewer. Finish with a bay leaf. Push together.

Put the kebabs under the grill or on to the barbecue and cook for about 8 minutes, turning twice, until the chicken is well browned and the figs singe at the edges. Serve sizzling hot. If you wish, boil the marinade while you are cooking the kebabs and pour a little over the kebabs just before you serve them.

Marinades
CRAFTY INGREDIENT

POULTRY

Indonesian Grilled Chicken

In Indonesia, chicken isn't quite as everyday a meat as it is in Britain so they're pretty careful with the leftovers. This recipe has a particularly delicious sauce that's spread on cooked, cold chicken and flashed under the grill. (You can buy whole, cooked chickens at extraordinarily good prices in every supermarket.) This is good with the Bitter Leafed Salad (see p. 25) and plain rice. It also goes very well with the Summer Salad Fried Rice (see p. 28).

time

20 mins

Serves 4

50 g (2 oz) ginger pieces in syrup
1 tablespoon ginger syrup (from the jar)
juice of 1 lemon
1 teaspoon chilli sauce
100 ml (3½ fl oz) soy sauce
1 teaspoon garlic purée
1 small roast chicken

Put the ginger, ginger syrup, lemon juice, chilli sauce, soy sauce and garlic purée in a food processor and blend until smooth. Joint the chicken, separating the leg joints and cutting the breasts in half. Discard the central carcass (or use to make stock).

Pre-heat the grill. Spread the ginger mixture on to the skin side of the chicken. Arrange the chicken pieces in the grill pan and grill for 6–7 minutes, until the chicken is hot and the sauce is bubbling and golden. (It is important to completely reheat the chicken.) Serve hot.

GINGER

● Ginger in syrup is a wonderful store cupboard standby. Apart from being used to add a slightly sweet and sour note to various savoury dishes, chopped up finely in its own syrup, it makes a wonderful sauce for vanilla ice-cream or it can be incorporated in a sponge pudding to give a fabulous ginger flavour.

POULTRY

Ginger
CRAFTY INGREDIENT

Wine with Poultry

Chicken and turkey are forgiving birds and virtually any wine goes, as long as the recipe is fairly plain. If you start to add things to poultry or put it in things, it can pose a real teaser.

Steely, leafy Chablis is excellent with rich, creamy, buttery sauces as its zingy acidity cuts neatly through the fat. Savoury, Chinese-style sauces, though, such as Michael's black and yellow bean recipes, call for wines with a smack of sweetness. A demi-sec fizz is fantastic.

Herby recipes, such as Michael's *Chicken with Smoked Garlic and Herb Tagliatelle* (see p.117) need wines laced with plenty of fruit and body so try spicy, mouth-filling New World Shiraz or creamy, lemony Australian Chardonnay.

As for Asian dishes, Alsace whites with a boost of spice, in particular Gewürztraminer, are tremendous. Yes, even with hot curries! Michael's *Chinese Barbecued Duck Breasts with Hoisin and Pancakes* (see p.122) is a smasher. The hoisin sauce is the most important element to match in this dish and, as such, a wine with sweet edges and a touch of spice is in order. A German Kabinett from Pfalz fits the bill perfectly but you could try a Riesling from New Zealand.

All-rounder Reds

Velvety, summer fruit-flavoured Pinot Noirs, simple red Burgundies or the more up-front styles from South Africa, Spain, Romania and even Argentina, dovetail well with poultry.

Italian reds also make delicious quaffing partners to poultry, especially Montepulciano d'Abruzzo with lashings of well-knit, sweet, marzipan-brambly-plummy flavours or deep, dense and spicy Primitivo.

New World reds set the appetite racing too, such as lavish Californian Zinfandel or a big, juicy, sun-filled Australian Cabernet Sauvignon.

All-rounder Whites

Turbo-charged Chardonnay blends couldn't be better and Australian Sémillon-Chardonnay is wonderful with its overtly sunny, toasty, fruit salad flavours. Poultry also takes kindly to the palate-cleansing punch of Sauvignon Blanc. Top choices include the vigorously zesty, flowering-currant-styled Sancerre, vibrant, grassy Sauvignon Blanc Vin de Pays d'Oc and the verdant, gooseberry-layered New Zealand styles.

Chicken Tortilla Pie

Chicken is a comparatively recent import to Mexican cooking, only brought over with the Spaniards, but tortillas, the flat Mexican cornbread, have been in existence for thousands of years. They make a surprisingly easy New World lasagne-style dish. The only hard part is waiting for it to finish cooking in the oven. It needs nothing with it, but is good followed by a salad.

time

30 mins

Serves 4

25 ml (1 fl oz) corn or sunflower oil

450 g (1 lb) stir-fry chicken pieces

1 red pepper, seeded and chopped

1 green pepper, seeded and chopped

250 g (9 oz) jar Napolitana-style tomato pizza topping

1 teaspoon chilli sauce, or more to taste

salt and freshly ground black pepper

1 packet of 8 soft wheat tortillas

100 g (4 oz) Cheddar or pizza cheese, grated

Pre-heat the oven to 200°C/400°F/Gas 6.

Heat the oil in a frying pan, add the chicken pieces and fry for about 5 minutes, until golden brown. Stir in the peppers, tomato pizza topping and chilli sauce. Mix well together and season generously with salt and pepper.

Using 2 tortillas, line the base of an oval or square baking dish measuring about 30 cm (12 inches). Spoon one-third of the chicken and tomato mixture on top of the tortilla layer, then layer another 2 tortillas and repeat, finishing with 2 tortillas at the top. Tuck in the sides so that the tortillas are inside the dish and sprinkle the cheese over the top.

Bake in the oven for 20 minutes, until it is hot throughout and the cheese has melted.

TORTILLAS

● Most of the tortillas you buy in Britain are made from wheat rather than corn, although the more authentic ones are also available.

● They're really excellent, whether eaten like a savoury pancake wrapped around meat or vegetables, or layered, as in this dish, or eaten as part of a recipe of *Sizzling Turkey Fajitas* (see p. 46).

● They make a great substitute for savoury pancakes if you're making a dish that calls for those.

POULTRY

Chicken with Smoked Garlic and Herb Tagliatelle

It's wonderful what they'll smoke these days and I don't mean in funny pipes. Smoked garlic is quite a new product but it's both interesting and surprisingly delicate. This dish is best eaten with some fresh herb-flavoured pasta with a little garlic to reinforce the flavour. It needs a green salad or a green vegetable to follow.

SMOKED GARLIC

● Smoked garlic, which can usually be found the vegetable section of your supermarket, is fresh garlic which has been cold smoked, usually as a whole head.

● It stores well in the fridge for up to a month.

● It can be used in many of the recipes in which fresh garlic is used, though it tends to go better with white meats and fish than with red meats.

● It's particularly good as part of an *Aïoli* or Garlic Mayonnaise.

Serves 4

25 g (1 oz) butter
25 ml (1 fl oz) vegetable oil
4 boneless chicken breasts, skinned and halved lengthways
250 g (9 oz) fresh herb and garlic tagliatelle
2 smoked garlic cloves, skinned
½ teaspoon salt
150 ml (5 fl oz) half-fat crème fraîche
1–2 teaspoons chopped fresh or frozen oregano

Heat the butter and oil in a frying pan, add the chicken pieces and fry over a medium heat for 10–12 minutes until golden brown.

Meanwhile, cook the tagliatelle in a large saucepan of boiling water for 4 minutes. Using the back of a knife or a teaspoon, crush the garlic with the salt.

Add the garlic mixture to the cooked chicken and stir quickly to coat. Add the crème fraîche, immediately remove from the heat and stir the cream through the juices in the pan to make a golden sauce. (Do not let the sauce come to the boil or it will separate.) Add the oregano.

Drain the tagliatelle, arrange as a nest on warmed serving plates and serve the chicken with its sauce in the centre.

Smoked Garlic
CRAFTY INGREDIENT

POULTRY

Black Bean Sauce
CRAFTY INGREDIENT

Chicken and Vegetable Stir-fry with Black Bean Sauce

Stir-fries can contain all kinds of weird and wonderful items but this one, except for the bean sprouts and the sauce, uses very ordinary, easily available British ingredients. The trick with all stir-fries is to get the pan really hot and not to put the oil in until that has happened. Once it has happened, do what the title tells you and stir all the time while it's frying. This is really good with plain cooked rice, perhaps following a bowl of chicken noodle or similar soup.

time

15 mins

Serves 4

I bunch spring onions, trimmed

I courgette

I tablespoon sunflower or corn oil

450 g (1 lb) stir-fry chicken strips or chicken breasts cut
    widthways into 1 cm (½ inch) strips

I teaspoon ginger purée

I garlic clove, crushed

I red pepper, seeded and cut into 5 mm (¼ inch) strips

100 g (4 oz) bean sprouts

160 g (6½ oz) jar black bean sauce

salt and freshly ground black pepper

Cut the spring onions into 7.5 cm (3 inch) lengths. If they are very fat, cut them in half lengthways. Using a potato peeler, peel ribbons off the courgette, turning it around until you come to the centre and discard.

Heat a wok or frying pan until really hot and just smoking. Pour in the oil, add the chicken, ginger and garlic and stir for about 5 minutes, until the chicken becomes opaque. Add the pepper and spring onions and cook for a further 3–5 minutes. Stir in the bean sprouts, black bean sauce and 100ml (3½ fl oz) water. Bring to the boil, stirring all the time. Season with salt and pepper and serve immediately.

BLACK BEAN SAUCE

● Black beans are small beans grown in China which are fermented, rather like soy beans for soy sauce, to create a textured and very savoury mixture. When you buy the sauce in jars it has already been processed in order to produce the lovely glossy finish to the stir-fry dishes in which you use it.

● It's good with beef and can be used as a key part of a marinade for barbecued meats.

Chicken Florentine

This Italian dish is so easy to make. It uses a ready made, fresh cheese sauce, now available from the chilled cabinet of the supermarket. Any flavour cheese sauce will do as long as it is not blue cheese — look out for one with Fontina cheese in it, if possible.

time

25 mins

Serves 4

4 boneless chicken breasts, skinned
500 ml (17 fl oz) chicken stock (made from a stock cube)
350 g (12 oz) frozen spinach, thawed or 750g (1½ lb) fresh spinach
15 g (½ oz) butter
a pinch of nutmeg
freshly ground black pepper
300 g (11 oz) tub fresh cheese sauce (for pasta)
2 tablespoons freshly grated Parmesan cheese

Pre-heat the grill. Place the chicken breasts in a saucepan pan with the chicken stock and poach for 15 minutes, or until tender.

Meanwhile, heat the frozen spinach and butter in a saucepan for 5 minutes. (If you are using fresh spinach, wash it well in cold water, removing any tough stalks. Blanch in boiling water for 2 minutes, then drain well and toss in melted butter.) Add the nutmeg and season with pepper.

Spread the cooked spinach over the base of a shallow, flameproof dish. Remove the cooked chicken from the saucepan and reserve 50 ml (2 fl oz) of the hot stock. Mix one-third of the cheese sauce with the reserved stock. Pour over the spinach and mix together. Place the chicken on top, spoon over the remaining sauce and sprinkle with Parmesan cheese. Grill for 5–6 minutes, until golden brown and bubbling. Serve hot.

FRESH CHEESE SAUCE

● Ready made, fresh cheese sauces are available in a variety of flavours. They come in tubs containing about 500 ml (17 fl oz) and, after being heated, can be simply poured on to hot cooked pasta, but they are also a marvellous base for a number of other dishes, not least for a *Quick Cheese Soufflé* (see p. 70).

● The flavours vary from quattro fromaggi, which contains four cheeses, to some quite specific ones based on individual cheeses. Choose one to suit the dish you're making.

Cheese Sauce
CRAFTY INGREDIENT

Turkey Spring Stew

There is a tradition of spring stews in France which are supposed to use lamb and baby vegetables but, in my experience, those are only ever available by the time summer arrives. However, with the kind of springs we tend to get, often cold and wet, we need a generous, but light, stew to warm up those chilly evenings and yet still leave us with hope of summer yet to come. This recipe is for one such stew. It's made with turkey pieces, that are now so widely available, and frozen vegetables, if they haven't yet arrived fresh in the shops. This needs no additional vegetables; just a little cheese and fruit to follow perhaps.

time

30 mins

Serves 4

2 tablespoons olive oil

450 g (1 lb) boneless turkey thigh meat, diced

450 g (1 lb) small new potatoes, scrubbed

250 g (9 oz) pickling onions, halved if large

salt and freshly ground black pepper

225 g (8 oz) prepared baby carrots

225 g (8 oz) frozen broad beans

225 g (8 oz) frozen peas

15 g (½ oz) cornflour

15 g (½ oz) butter

chopped fresh marjoram or parsley, to garnish

In a large saucepan, heat the oil and gently fry the turkey for 2–3 minutes. Meanwhile, cut any large potatoes into similar sized pieces to the meat. Stir into the pan, add the onions and season well with salt and pepper. Add the carrots, cover with about 1 litre (1¾ pints) boiling water and simmer for 15–20 minutes. Stir in the beans and peas and simmer for a further 2 minutes.

Meanwhile, mash together the cornflour and butter. Over a low heat, stir forkfuls of the butter mixture into the stew until it melts and thickens as it returns to the boil. Serve immediately, in soup bowls or on warmed serving plates, sprinkled with fresh marjoram or parsley to garnish.

POULTRY

FROZEN VEGETABLES

● Frozen peas and broad beans are often regarded rather contemptuously in Britain but they are usually very good-quality vegetables blanched and frozen at the peak of their condition. It's the way they are cooked afterwards that often affects them most severely. Cooking them in something like a stew, very lightly so that their bright colour and good texture can add to the quality of the dish, is ideal.

● Another way to get the best out of these vegetables is not to cook them in water but in a knob of butter with a teaspoon of the appropriate herb, such as savoury for beans and fresh mint for peas. By this method, as they melt from frozen they produce enough liquid to cook themselves perfectly in 2–3 minutes.

Baked Chicken with Yellow Bean Sauce

Although the flavours in this dish are Eastern, the methodology is quite European and is best, therefore, served with European-style vegetables. In fact, I'm extremely fond of it with mashed potatoes, and new potatoes are fine too. It's good to have some vegetables with contrasting colours, such as bright green, crisp, Stir-Tossed Caraway Cabbage (see p. 96) and Carrots with Star Anise (see p. 97) glazed with a little butter and sugar.

time

30 mins

Serves 4

4 part boned chicken breasts
1 teaspoon garlic salt
juice of 1 lime
4 tablespoons yellow bean sauce

Pre-heat the oven to 220°C/425°F/Gas 7.

Place the chicken breasts in a baking dish into which they will all just fit. Add 150ml (5 fl oz) boiling water and sprinkle with the garlic salt. Mix together the lime juice and yellow bean sauce and carefully spread over the chicken breasts, covering as much of the chicken skin as you can.

Cook in the oven for 25 minutes, until tender. Serve the chicken breasts on warmed plates with the sauce poured over the top.

● Yellow beans are another of the flavouring ingredients that come from China and have only recently reached our shores. Once again, they are now available in supermarkets on the speciality shelves and in Chinese and Far Eastern shops. The European packaging tends to be in glass jars but in Chinese shops you may find the original tins.

● It's excellent spread on a whole chicken before roasting.

● It's also used to stir-fry other meats, generally with the addition of cashew nuts.

Yellow Bean Sauce
CRAFTY INGREDIENT

Chinese Barbecued Duck Breasts with Hoisin and Pancakes

Since the advent of northern Chinese-style food, duck with pancakes has become a firm favourite in restaurants. However a whole Peking Duck takes a long time to prepare. This method enables you to achieve the same combination of flavours and textures much faster. The hoisin sauce is a thick, pungent, barbecue flavoured, soy-based sauce and is the traditional accompaniment. All the ingredients should be available in any supermarket.

time

25 mins

BARBARY DUCK BREASTS

● Barbary ducks are a different species from the Aylesbury or white feathered ducks that we're used to and, while they're not essential to this dish, they do have the advantage of being larger, leaner and better flavoured. The species of duck they come from is more akin to the wild duck and the benefits are obvious.

● If you fancy making a French *Magret de Canard*, they grill perfectly on their own with a little lemon juice and olive oil spread over them. They then need slicing thinly before serving.

● They cook extremely well in a pan (skin side down to start with, to produce the cooking fat) with 2–3 tablespoons of good-quality marmalade stirred in with a cup of water, to make a marvellous bitter orange sauce.

Serves 4

1 tablespoon runny honey
1 tablespoon soy sauce
4 Barbary duck breasts

To serve:
10 cm (4 inch) piece of cucumber
4 spring onions
100 ml (3½ fl oz) hoisin sauce
2 packets Chinese pancakes, each containing 10 pancakes

Pre-heat the grill. Mix together the honey and soy sauce and use to coat the Barbary duck breasts. Leave for about 5 minutes. Cook under a hot grill for 8–10 minutes on each side, starting with the flesh side and finishing with the skin side, until crisp and brown.

Meanwhile, cut the cucumber in half lengthways, scoop out the seeds and cut lengthways into matchstick-sized pieces. Shred the spring onions and put them on 2 serving plates. Pour the hoisin sauce into a bowl. Heat the pancakes, either in a colander standing over a saucepan of boiling water or under the switched off grill when the duck has just finished cooking.

Using a very sharp knife, slice the duck breasts widthways into 5 mm (¼ inch) slices. To eat, spread a little hoisin sauce on to a pancake, sprinkle on a few strips of cucumber and spring onions, add a few slices of duck and roll up the pancake. This is best eaten with your fingers.

MEAT

Despite the current scares and general decline in the sale of red meat, it's still, for those of us who are carnivores, the basis of very appealing meals. The general trend seems to be to eat red meat less often but, when you do, look for high quality. If there's been one real benefit from the BSE scare it has been that the sourcing and handling of beef in particular, but other meat as well, has improved enormously as the chain of responsibility has been established extremely clearly by all the supermarkets and most good butchers. Alongside this, to encourage people to eat more meat and to accommodate smaller families, the selection of prepared portions has greatly increased. All meats can now be bought in steaks and fillets, often seasoned and flavoured, particularly in the summer for barbecues.

Tougher joints are tenderized and a lot of meat is now sold in what is usually called 'traditional' style which means that it has been properly hung to achieve the tenderness and flavour that we remember. Many butchers and supermarkets now sell meat that has a specific source or origin, Aberdeen Angus for example, or from an organic farm or supplier. This is often worth seeking out because, although it is more expensive, not only is its safety guaranteed but the quality is usually far higher than other meat.

Don't forget game in this context. Venison, in particular, has begun to be farmed very widely in Britain and is both high quality and relatively cheap, compared with beef. It also has the advantage of being naturally low in fat and high in flavour.

LAMB FILLETS

● Neck lamb fillets are the eye of what used to be called neck chops, boned out of the meat and making a delicious and simple, if elongated, form of lamb steak. As well as being cooked whole, as in this recipe, they're excellent cut into pieces for kebabs, sliced thinly across the grain in stir-fries and used in chunks as the basis of a really delicious lamb casserole.

● They're quite fatty as well as meaty and benefit from cooking with as little extra fat as possible.

Lamb Fillets with Fennel and Leeks

The combination of lamb and leeks is a traditional Celtic one, indeed more especially Welsh, but the addition of fennel, the large bulbous aniseed relation to celery, produces a light and extraordinarily interestingly textured stir-fry. Some quick-cooked noodles, tossed in a little butter, go well with this recipe.

time

20 mins

Serves 4

2 tablespoons vegetable oil
½ teaspoon crushed garlic
450 g (1 lb) leeks, cut into 5 mm (¼ inch) thick slices
1 large fennel head, cut into 5 mm (¼ inch) thick slices
salt and freshly ground black pepper
450 g (1 lb) lamb neck fillets
½ teaspoon chopped fresh or frozen marjoram,
½ teaspoon chopped fresh or frozen thyme,

Heat the oil in a frying pan or wok until just below smoking point. Add the garlic and immediately add the leeks and fennel, stirring and tossing them together for 5–6 minutes, until well cooked but not totally wilted.

Meanwhile, in a separate frying pan, sprinkle a little salt into the pan and heat until the salt starts to brown. Add the lamb fillets and dry-fry for 2–3 minutes. Turn and cook for a further 3–4 minutes if you like your lamb slightly pink or 5–7 minutes if you like your lamb more thoroughly cooked. Just before the lamb has finished cooking, sprinkle with the herbs. Pile the vegetables on to a warmed serving dish and serve the lamb fillets on top. More salt is unlikely to be needed but black pepper goes well.

MEAT

Lamb Fillets
CRAFTY INGREDIENT

Roast Butterfly of Lamb with a Moroccan Sauce

A leg of lamb, boned and prepared in a butterfly shape cooks extremely quickly and retains most of its natural juice. I've suggested a version here with a Moroccan sauce which combines both fresh herbs and quite a powerful chilli spicing. It's possible to bone the lamb yourself, but it's also quite easy to get your butcher or supermarket to do it for you if you give them at least 24 hours notice.

time

30 mins

Serves 6

1.5 kg (3 lb) leg of lamb, boned
2 tablespoons tomato purée
2 teaspoons chilli purée
1 teaspoon ground cumin
2 tablespoons chopped fresh or frozen mint
150 ml (5 fl oz) natural yoghurt
cooked rice or couscous, to serve

Cut through the meaty part of the lamb until you're about 2.5 cm (1 inch) from the skin, then fold the joint outwards. You'll find you have a butterfly-shaped piece of meat which should be between 2.5–4 cm (1–1½ inches) thick all the way across.

Pre-heat the grill to its highest setting. Mix together the tomato purée, chilli purée, cumin and 1 tablespoon of mint. Spread the mixture on both sides of the lamb and leave to marinate for 1–2 minutes, while the grill is heating. Place the meat on the grid of the grill pan with about 100 ml (3½ fl oz) water in the pan underneath. Grill about 2.5 cm (1 inch) away from the grill element for about 12 minutes on each side. If you like your meat well done you may want to add 5 minutes.

Remove the meat from the heat and leave to stand in the warm. Stir the remaining fresh mint into the yoghurt and add the pan juices, to taste. If there are a lot of juices you may only want to add a little, but if they've reduced to a small amount, most should be added to the yoghurt. Slice the meat thickly, pour over the sauce, and serve with rice or couscous.

FRESH MINT

● Fresh mint used to be something that everyone had in their gardens but, with the demise of herb gardens, the benefit of having it available in supermarkets, both growing in little pots, fresh and prepacked, is enormous.
● It can, of course, be used for mint sauce but it is also delicious with the leaves torn up into salads, particularly those with a creamy dressing.
● It's great chopped with spring onions and parsley and mixed into a rice or bulgar salad.
● It works surprisingly well when used with grilled fish, particularly with a solid meaty fish like monkfish, as they do in the south of Italy.

MEAT

Oz WINE · Wine with Red Meat

Well, let's get on with it! Time to break out those bottles of red wine with breeding, body, tannin, generous ripe fruit, gentle maturity and harmony.

Beef

Yummy recipes call for yummy wines! Impressive clarets? Enormous Californian Cabernet Sauvignons? Blockbusting Aussie Shiraz? Yes, yes and yes. However, demure, high-class red Burgundies will go equally well with Michael's steak recipes. The coleslaw with the *Chicken Fried Steak* (see p.129) may prove a bit of a problem – but it's worth the risk!

You'll need to gamble a little more with the *Gourmet Cheeseburger* (see p. 132) though – the meat, tomato and peppered cheese are a medley of contrasting tastes. Bright, fruity, young red Rioja or spicy Californian Zinfandel are good foils to these flavours.

When it comes to *Beef Frikadellers with Mango Chutney* (see p. 130), I'm going to bend a rule. Yes, it's red meat but the Thai flavours demand a rich, oaky, dry *white* wine. Go for a good Chardonnay from Australia or California.

Lamb

This glorious meat is delicate, succulent and sweet. Served plain, it goes brilliantly with practically any full-bodied Cabernet Sauvignon. For the ultimate, choose a classic Médoc or a big, forward style, spilling over with warm blackberry-cassis fruit and cedar flavours, from Australia's Médoc – Coonawarra. Cahors and Portuguese Bairrada Garrafeira are excellent budget choices.

Spice needs spice, so when it comes to Michael's *Roast Butterfly of Lamb with a Moroccan Sauce* (see opposite) go for a Californian Gewürztraminer. The *Lamb Fillets with Fennel and Leeks* (see p.125) dish, though, needs bolstering firmness and acidity – an Italian Barbera works well.

Venison

Go for elegance on a grand scale – Cabernets from Bordeaux or California are marvellous. Alternatively, try a spicy blockbuster from the Rhône such as Châteauneuf-du-Pape, Hermitage, Gigondas – the best you can afford!

Steak in a Cream Sauce

This is a dish that's cooked in moments and always welcome. It is a technique I learnt many years ago from that doyenne of cookery writers, Elizabeth David. She used it for veal but it works well with almost any meat or fish. Adjust flavourings and cooking times to suit the key ingredient but the basic cream sauce mixture is the same for all of them. As I'm cooking steak I have used the delicious French Dijon mustard which goes so well with red meats. This dish is traditionally served with French fries but it's also particularly good with mashed potatoes which act as a wonderful absorber for the cream sauce.

time

10 mins

Serves 4

25 ml (1 fl oz) vegetable oil

4 sirloin steaks, each weighing 175–225 g (6–8 oz)

salt and freshly ground black pepper

250 ml (8 fl oz) double cream or crème fraîche

1 tablespoon smooth Dijon mustard

1 teaspoon chopped fresh parsley

Heat a frying pan, into which all the steaks will fit until hot. Add the oil, swirl it round and immediately add the steaks, unseasoned. They may stick to the pan for 30–40 seconds but don't be tempted to loosen them as they will come loose in their own time. Cook for 2–3 minutes, turn and cook for another 1–2 minutes for rare, 2 minutes for medium and 3–4 minutes for well done. Season with salt and pepper and transfer to warmed serving plates. Pour the double cream or crème fraîche into the pan, bring to the boil, then stir in the mustard and scrape in all the sediments on the bottom of the pan. Add the parsley. Pour the sauce over the steaks and serve immediately.

DIJON MUSTARD

● French mustards are very good to cook with because of their milder and more herb-based flavours. They come in a wide variety, from pale gold and quite pungent Dijon, through the grain mustards from Meux, to the darker and much more herby mustards from Bordeaux.

● In addition to being used just to season food, they go extremely well with cream sauces, white and cheese sauces and as barbecue marinades.

● The golden varieties are very good spread on slices of French bread which are then used to top (mustard side down) a stew in the form of a cobbler.

MEAT

Chicken Fried Steak

The wonderful title of this recipe comes from America and means a piece of beef coated in the egg and breadcrumb coating used for southern fried chicken. It's an excellent way of making the very thin cut, but delicious, tenderized minute steaks more substantial. This should be served with mashed potatoes and a coleslaw salad to balance the richness of the meat dish.

time

20 mins

Serves 4

2 thick slices of fresh white bread, made into breadcrumbs
½ teaspoon chopped fresh or frozen rosemary
½ teaspoon chopped fresh or frozen oregano
4 tenderized frying steaks each weighing about 100 g (4 oz) and
    5 mm – 1 cm (¼-½ inch) thick
juice of ½ lemon
50 g (2 oz) plain white flour
1 egg
100 ml (3½ fl oz) cooking oil

Mix together the breadcrumbs, rosemary and oregano and put on a plate. Dip the steaks into the lemon juice and then shake them in a bag with the flour. Beat the egg and put it into a deep plate or soup bowl. Dip each steak into the egg, shake off any surplus and coat with the breadcrumbs. Leave the steaks to stand for 2–3 minutes. Heat the oil in a large frying pan into which the steaks will fit in one layer (you may find you need to do this in 2 batches). Add the steaks and fry for 5–6 minutes on each side, until crisp and golden. (Do not let them go dark brown or they will become very tough.) Serve hot.

PRE-TENDERIZED STEAK

● This is achieved by a sophisticated machine, (not by beating the steaks in the old fashioned sense) which presses the steaks between boards containing very small sharp knives and cuts the long, tough, chewy fibres in the meat. The result is 'tenderized' meat at a very reasonable price. You can, if you wish, bang the steaks a little with a meat tenderizing hammer but the difference it makes is comparatively small.

● Tenderized steaks make excellent quick-fried or flash-fried steak with various sauces, such as mushroom, or they can be cut into strips for stroganoffs or stir-fries.

Steak
CRAFTY INGREDIENT

MEAT

Beef Frikadellers with Mango Chutney

Frikadeller is the word that is universally used in the Scandinavian region for meatballs. It's occasionally used in northern Germany as well. What distinguishes these northern European meatballs from their southern counterparts tends to be their smaller size and strong spicy flavouring. This recipe includes a quite delicious set of tropical flavours to go with the meatballs.

time

30 mins

Serves 4

500 g (18 oz) lean minced beef

100 g (4 oz) onion, very finely chopped

3 tablespoons Thai coriander, coconut and lime sauce

1 tablespoon chopped fresh or frozen dill

1 egg, beaten

salt and freshly ground black pepper

2 tablespoons vegetable oil

4 tablespoons mango chutney

boiled potatoes and green vegetables, to serve

In a large bowl, mix together the beef, onion, Thai sauce, dill and the egg.

Season generously with salt and pepper and knead by hand until well blended. Divide the mixture in half, divide again in half and keep dividing until you have 16 separate pieces. Wet your hands and roll each piece into a round meatball.

In a large frying pan, heat the oil and fry the meatballs, turning 2–3 times, for 10–12 minutes, until they are well browned on the outside but still juicy inside. Remove the meatballs from the pan and stir the mango chutney into the juices. If there are any large chunks in the mango chutney, chop them up.

Stir in 125 ml (4 fl oz) water, bring to the boil and stir until all the sediment on the bottom of the pan has been mixed into the sauce. Pour over the meatballs and serve with potatoes and green vegetables.

BOTTLED SAUCES

● Lea and Perrins are to be congratulated on having recently developed a number of very interesting and useful sauce combinations, in bottles the same shape as Worcestershire sauce. As well as coriander, coconut and lime, there is a ginger sauce, several chilli sauces and a simple purée of garlic. They form a marvellously easy base for a quick stir-fry of meat, fish or vegetables. They're also good because they're quite pungent – a little goes a long way.

MEAT

Oz WINE Lookalikes

Let's face it, we all get bored. Bored with our job. Bored with dog-walking. Bored with our football team always losing. So, there's no reason why we shouldn't get bored with our favourite wine too. How often do you yearn to try something different? But where should you start?

Tight Purse Strings

You don't have to spend one extra penny! One of the joys of living in the UK is the unique breadth and range of wines that we can buy. So, if your favourite wine costs £3.99, you can easily bet your last £3.99 that there'll be an abundance of lookalikes in the same price bracket.

Trading Up

Talking of price, one way of reviving flagging tastebuds is to spend a little more. It is generally true to say that the more you pay, the better the wine. The best way to do this is to learn a bit of label lore (see pp. 150–152) and work out if your favourite wine fits into any classification system – and then buy the next grade up.

Take Rioja, for example. Basic Rioja is pretty good but try upgrading to Reserva or, better still, top-of-the-class Gran Reserva. You'll enjoy the same sort of flavours, but taste the difference in intensity and personality!

Flavour Trails and Globetrotting

If you think about it carefully, you'll soon realize that there's usually one significantly pleasurable taste in your favourite wine. It could be blackcurrants or greengages, spice or buttered toast. Unless it's an oaky taste, which is a direct result of winemaking practice, more often than not it's the grape that gives the primary flavour. It helps if you can put a favourite fruit flavour to a grape variety – if you like gooseberries, for example, you're bound to enjoy anything from Sauvignon Blanc.

It's easy. Identify the grape and you're laughing all the way down the wine aisles. Kick off with another wine from the same grape from the same country. Crack that and you can then move on to new countries.

Gourmet Cheeseburger

A well-made hamburger is a real pleasure, especially if they're made thick enough to still be juicy in the middle after cooking. A gourmet cheeseburger, however, needs a better cheese than just the pre-processed sliced variety. This recipe provides an excellent way of turning hamburgers into really special cheeseburgers. It uses Boursin, that fabulous French peppered cheese, that's widely available throughout Britain these days. Serve them as you would any cheeseburger, in a bun with relishes and a little lettuce and tomato, or you can, if you like, serve them with potatoes and vegetables.

time

20 mins

Serves 4

500 g (18 oz) lean minced beef
50 g (2 oz) onion, very finely chopped
2 tablespoons tomato ketchup
1 egg yolk
125 g (4½ oz) Boursin peppered cream cheese

Pre-heat the grill. Put the beef, onion, tomato sauce and egg yolk into a large bowl and mash well together with a fork. Divide into 4 pieces and shape into 10–13 cm (4–5 inch) patties. Grill the patties for 2 minutes on each side for rare and 3 minutes on each side for medium. Meanwhile, mash the Boursin cheese. Spread 1 tablespoon of the cheese over each cooked burger and return to the grill for no more than 1 minute, until the cheese bubbles and melts. Serve hot.

PEPPERED BOURSIN

● Boursin and other cream cheeses are essentially very mild, smooth, lactic-based cheeses, but they carry other flavours brilliantly. The peppered style comes in two forms, one with the peppers mixed through it and one with the cheese coated with coarsely crushed peppercorns. Depending on how much you like pepper, either version is suitable for this or any other recipe. The crushed pepper variety has more of an impact.
● Mixed with a little milk or single cream, they make excellent dips for crudités and crisps and also blend very well into salad dressings. Use a food processor or liquidizer to make sure the dressing is smooth.

MEAT

ROWAN AND QUINCE JELLY

● In the last few years, the selection of jams in our grocers and supermarkets has improved vastly. Lower sugar, higher fruit content, the use of whole fruit and a wider variety of flavours have been enormously beneficial. There is a Continental influence as well, providing jams with a slightly softer texture.

● Most interesting of all has been the revival of some of the old-fashioned preserves and jellies, including quince, which is a dark, deep red coloured jelly and rowan, which comes from the berries of the ash tree and is bright orange.

● Both these jellies have a degree of sharpness and astringency which makes them really sweet and sour. They are perfect not only for adding to game but also for glazing apple tarts and eating on sweet breads or scones.

Rowan Jelly
CRAFTY INGREDIENT

Fruit Glazed Venison

Venison, like so many other foods, now seems to be available in portions that were unheard of a few years ago and, in addition, the supermarkets appear to be stocking it with a vengeance. This is a good thing because, not only is it one of the most deliciously flavoured meats available, it's also low in fat and cholesterol. This recipe takes advantage of perhaps the most expensive form of game meat, which is venison steaks, and teams it with a lovely old-fashioned English fruit flavour to make a quick and delicious dish for the autumn or winter.

time

15 mins

Serves 4

25 ml (1 fl oz) vegetable oil
25 g (1 oz) butter
4 venison steaks, each weighing about 175 g (6 oz)
100 g (4 oz) onion, finely chopped
150 ml (5 fl oz) double cream or crème fraîche
2 tablespoons quince or rowan jelly
salt and freshly ground black pepper
boiled potatoes and vegetables, to serve

In a heavy-based frying pan heat the oil and butter, swirling the butter around until it stops sizzling. Add the steaks and fry for 3–4 minutes on each side, depending on their thickness. When you turn the steaks, add the chopped onion, stir in about 100 ml (3 ½ fl oz) water and continue to cook over a high heat. When the steaks are cooked, stir in the cream and quince or rowan jelly and continue to cook over a medium heat until the jelly has melted and the cream and pan juices have blended together. Season and serve the steaks immediately with potatoes and vegetables.

MEAT

133

Oz WINE Cooking with Wine

Would you slosh a thirty pound bottle of wine into a casserole? No! In the old days, however, maxim decreed that you cooked with the wine you were about to drink, so if you fancied a treat with your Boeuf Bourguignon…!

Thanks to the biochemical boffins, we now know that we can throw any wine into the pot. It's quite okay to use leftovers, sediment and even a dodgy, vinegary wine. Like alcohol, volatile compounds that sour the taste of drinking wine are driven off within 15 minutes of cooking.

The important thing to remember is that a wine's richness is going to concentrate with every simmering second. So, if you use an elaborately oaky wine, you'll end up with a lot of woody flavours. Similarly, a wine of high acidity will give a nippy, piquant taste to the finished dish.

Wine casts other spells in the kitchen apart from in the hotpot. It's a great tenderizer in marinades and there's no limit to what you can do to soups, sauces and gravies with a drop – well, maybe three! –of wine. You can also perk up a salad dressing by tossing in the odd splash of wine or better still, make your own wine vinegar.

Let's not forget the puddings. Where would a Sherry trifle be without the Sherry or a Zabaglione without the Marsala? A dash of sweet wine can transform any fruit salad. Or do what the Bordelaise do and splash some red wine over strawberries…mmm…a divine combination!

If disaster strikes and your work of culinary art turns out to be a bit too winey, you can always soften it by adding cream. Glory be! Yet another notch loosened in the old belt…!

Tips

● For handy stand-bys, boil leftover wines until reduced by half and freeze in ice cube trays or yoghurt pots.

● Don't use aluminium pots and pans when cooking with wine – the wine reacts with the aluminium and causes discolouration to the food.

● If you're also using cream in your recipes, make sure that the wine is added first. Doing it the other way around makes your sauce curdle.

Wild Rice

WILD RICE AND BASMATI MIX

● This is now sold both as a branded product and as an own brand in many supermarkets. It's a mix of North American 'wild' or 'black' rice, specially treated so that it cooks for the same time as the high-quality long-grain Basmati.

● The wild rice adds a nutty texture to the already first-class flavour and size of the Basmati rice and makes it a spectacular accompaniment to all sorts of food. It's not really suitable for Indian or Chinese dishes but better accompanying European casseroles or pan-fried dishes.

● It makes a good salad, particularly with added nuts. In America it is often used in soups, instead of potatoes or cornflour as an unusual thickener.

Venison and Wild Rice Stir-fry

Venison steaks are probably best for this dish as I haven't yet seen venison sold in stir-fry packs. Although the recipe is a quick and easy stir-fry, both the ingredients and final effect are sufficiently grand to make this dish very acceptable at dinner parties.

time

25 mins

Serves 4

275 g (10 oz) wild rice and Basmati mix
2 tablespoons vegetable oil
15 g (½ oz) butter
750 g (1½) lb venison steak, cut into 5 mm (¼ inch) slices
1 garlic clove, crushed, or 1 teaspoon garlic purée
225 g (8 oz) onions, cut into 5 mm (¼ inch) slices
225 g (8 oz) green peppers, cut into 5 mm (¼ inch) slices
225 g (8 oz) chestnut mushrooms, cut into 5 mm (¼ inch) slices
salt and freshly ground black pepper
300 ml (10 fl oz) sour cream
1 tablespoon chopped fresh or frozen parsley, to garnish

Measure the rice in a jug, then put in a saucepan with twice its volume of cold water. Add a pinch of salt and a drop of oil, bring to the boil, cover and simmer over the lowest possible heat for 12–15 minutes, until the water has been absorbed.

Meanwhile, heat the oil and butter in a large frying pan, add the venison, then fry quickly on both sides to seal. Stir in the garlic and onions and cook for 5 minutes. Add the peppers and mushrooms and cook for a further 5 minutes.

When the rice is cooked, put a sheet of kitchen paper across the top of the pan, replace the lid and leave to stand.

Season the venison generously with salt and pepper and, over a high heat, stir in the sour cream, tossing together until the cream is hot. Turn the rice into a warmed serving bowl and stir lightly with a fork to break up into individual grains. Add the venison stir-fry and serve sprinkled with the parsley.

MEAT

135

PASTA AND NOODLES

Both the Chinese and Italians claim to have invented pasta. There are unquestionably recipes, and indeed some paintings and drawings, that suggest that pasta was being eaten in Italy as far back as Roman times. Either way, what's interesting is the great variety of dishes in which pasta can be used. The recipes I've given here reflect both the Eastern and the Western traditions and some slightly unusual ways of cooking it.

Today, we have the choice of using fresh or dried pasta. Over the past few years a whole range of fresh pastas have arrived in our supermarkets that will keep for several days if kept chilled in the fridge. As well as the more well-known types, such as spaghetti and tagliatelle, there are the stuffed pastas that come with a variety of fillings, with cheese, mushrooms and spinach being the most popular. There are also a number of versions of fresh Chinese or Far Eastern pastas available, generally known as noodles, which are often thinner and flatter than the Western varieties. All fresh pasta cooks extremely quickly; even the stuffed varieties need only 5 or 6 minutes.

Dried pasta offers a wider range of varieties: plain pasta, made with wheat and water; egg pasta; and pastas flavoured and coloured with tomatoes and spinach. There are also pastas containing herbs and garlic in both traditional and wholewheat forms. If you're buying European pasta, make sure it's made in Italy as they use very hard durum wheat which gives it more substance when cooked. Dried pasta is an excellent storecupboard product and will keep for up to 4 months if kept in an airtight container.

To go with modern pastas, there have emerged in the shops a whole range of sauces to support them. However, it's also very easy to make quick fresh sauces of your own for pasta. Remember too, as with rice, that good pasta is often eaten in it's countries of origin very simply. In Italy, for example, a large knob of butter or a tablespoon or two of good olive oil, a handful of chopped herbs and some freshly grated Parmesan cheese is often all that's eaten with first class pasta.

Rice Noodles
CRAFTY INGREDIENT

RICE NOODLES

● These noodles, which look
as though they've had a perm,
are very similar in many ways
to European egg noodles.
They're excellent precooked
and then stir-fried with other
ingredients to make a fried
noodle dish, or cooked plainly
as an alternative to rice with a
combination of Chinese
dishes.

● Rice noodles are the
original ingredient added to a
rich chicken stock, with a few
sliced spring onions, to make
Chicken Noodle Soup.

Crispy Noodles with Crab Foo Yung

*Foo Yung is a kind of Chinese omelette made predominantly of egg whites.
This combination of crispy noodles and crab is something I learnt in
Chinatown, Soho. It's an extraordinary combination of flavours and textures
and can be served on its own as a surprisingly substantial lunch, as a light
snack dish or as part of a larger Chinese meal.*

time

30 mins

Serves 4

vegetable oil, for deep frying
4 tablespoons cooking oil (not olive oil)
I bunch of spring onions, finely chopped
I teaspoon crushed or puréed garlic
I teaspoon crushed or puréed ginger
225g (8 oz) fresh or frozen white crab meat
2 tablespoons light soy sauce
I egg yolk and 3 egg whites
half a 250 g (9 oz) packet of rice noodles

Heat the oil for deep frying. To make the crab mixture for the omelette,
heat 2 tablespoons oil in a frying pan, add the spring onions, garlic and
ginger and fry for I minute. Add the crab meat, soy sauce and egg yolk.

Whisk the egg whites until stiff but not dry. Break each sheet of
noodles in half and very carefully drop each sheet individually into the
hot oil. (The noodles should not be precooked.) Within 30 seconds
they will expand into a solid mass of crispy cooked noodles. Remove
immediately from the oil and allow to drain thoroughly on kitchen
paper. Using a 15–18 cm (7–8 inch) frying pan, heat the remaining
2 tablespoons of oil and fry the egg whites, turning them quickly but
trying not to lose all the air. Add the crab mixture and stir together,
then cook over a low to medium heat for 2–3 minutes, until the bottom
is set but the middle slightly soft.

Arrange the cooked noodles on a warmed serving dish, breaking
them up if necessary to fit on the dish. Slide the omelette on top and
serve, cut into wedges, with the noodles.

PASTA AND NOODLES

137

Tagliatelle with Peas and Smoked Salmon

This is a very elegant version of pasta that was developed in a famous restaurant in Rome. There they used the Italian raw ham, prosciutto, but I find that using smoked salmon produces a lighter dish; smoked salmon is also more readily available in this country. It's not only delicious but also extremely pretty to look at. Served in small portions, on elegant plates, it makes a wonderful starter for a special dinner party.

time

25 mins

Serves 6 as a starter or 4 as a main dish

175 g (6 oz) fresh or frozen (not minted) peas

350 g (12 oz) egg tagliatelle

25 ml (1 fl oz) cooking oil

175 ml (6 fl oz) crème fraîche

50 g (2 oz) butter

175 g (6 oz) smoked salmon trimmings

salt

If using fresh peas, cook in boiling water for about 10 minutes, until tender, then drain.

Put the tagliatelle into a large saucepan of boiling, salted water with the oil. Boil for 3 minutes, remove from the heat, cover and leave to stand for 7 minutes.

Meanwhile, put the crème fraîche and butter in a small saucepan and bring to the boil, stirring until the butter melts. Add the fresh or frozen peas.

Slice any large salmon trimmings into matchstick-length pieces and add two-thirds to the cream sauce. Bring to the boil and bubble for a moment. Drain the pasta, return to the pan and thoroughly stir in the cream sauce. Serve on 4 warmed plates and sprinkle the remaining smoked salmon trimmings over the top.

SMOKED SALMON TRIMMINGS

● You can of course make this dish with whole slices of smoked salmon but these days you can always find packets of smoked salmon trimmings, which are the offcuts. They taste just the same and, for cooking purposes, are ideal.

● They make a lovely filling for a quick omelette; go well tossed in a little butter for no more than a minute with scrambled eggs; and, cooked under a hot grill for no more than 1 minute a side they make a lovely addition to a Salad Niçoise instead of tuna.

PASTA AND NOODLES

Smoked Salmon
CRAFTY INGREDIENT

138

Pasta Shells with Blue Cheese Sauce

In Britain we tend to think of cheese sauces as pale and creamy but in fact blue cheese makes a very interesting ingredient. In this recipe, which contains possibly the easiest cheese sauce ever made, blue cheese is teamed with pasta shells, known in Italy as conchiglie. *This is a fridge and store cupboard dish so the ingredients are always to hand but it is no less delicious for that. It makes a good pasta starter to an Italian meal and is also a quite substantial dish in its own right in generous proportions.*

time

20 mins

Serves 4

350 g (12 oz) pasta shells

salt

150 g (5 oz) Italian blue-veined cheese such as Dolcelatte or
    Gorgonzola

25 g (1 oz) butter

150 ml (5 fl oz) double cream

2 tablespoons freshly grated Parmesan cheese

1 tablespoon chopped fresh or frozen parsley

Put the pasta in a large saucepan of boiling, salted water. Return to the boil, then boil for 3 minutes. Cover, remove from the heat and leave to stand for 7 minutes.

Meanwhile, mash the cheese with the butter. Pour the cream into a non-stick saucepan and add the cheese mixture, spoonful by spoonful, stirring over a moderate heat to let the cheese mixture to melt into the hot cream. When all the cheese has melted, allow it to bubble for a moment, then remove from the heat.

When the pasta has been standing for 7 minutes, drain and turn into a large, warmed serving bowl. Pour over the blue cheese sauce and toss to mix well together. Sprinkle with the Parmesan cheese, then the parsley, and serve immediately.

PASTA AND NOODLES

ITALIAN BLUE CHEESE PORTIONS

● These days the Italians, like everybody else, are marketing their cheese in pre-portioned packets as well as in whole rounds and drums. There are two or three varieties available: mountain and plains Gorgonzola (the former being slightly saltier) and Dolcellate, which is a milder form of Gorgonzola.

● Apart from cooking, they make excellent additions crumbled into salads, particularly with walnuts or crunchy croûtons to contrast with the creamy texture.

● They make a delicious cheese and chutney sandwich but you need to use a chutney that has a reasonable amount of sweetness to it. They also make a lovely topping for an unusual gratin, particularly winter vegetables.

Blue Cheese

CRAFTY INGREDIENT

Greek Yoghurt
CRAFTY INGREDIENT

Macaroni Pastitsio

Pastitsio is a Greek name for what often seems more of an Italian dish. It's a very simple, quick way of making a layered baked pasta dish. This is a vegetarian version. If you want to, you could add meat and make a Bolognese Sauce (see p. 143) but without adding the cream.

see p. 143

time

30 mins

GREEK YOGHURT

● Greek yoghurt is full-cream milk yoghurt which has been strained to allow some of the liquid to drain out. It's therefore very thick and creamy. It's excellent for cooking because of this thickness and is super for making curries.

● It's good stirred into hot soups where you might have used sour cream or as an additional ingredient. It's particularly good with a colourful one such as Broccoli Soup.

● It also makes delicious, quick puddings, especially with a little Greek honey stirred in and a few walnuts sprinkled on top.

Serves 4

25 g (8 oz) macaroni

4 tablespoons olive oil

225 g (8 oz) onions, chopped

225 g (8 oz) carrots, cut into 5 mm (¼ inch) slices

225 g (8 oz) courgettes, cut into 5 mm (¼ inch) pieces

2 celery sticks, cut into 5 mm (¼ inch) pieces

1 teaspoon crushed garlic

1 tablespoon tomato purée

420 g (14 oz) can chopped Italian tomatoes

1 teaspoon fresh or frozen thyme

1 teaspoon fresh or frozen oregano

salt and freshly ground black pepper

2 eggs, beaten

150 ml (5 fl oz) Greek natural yoghurt

Pre-heat the oven to 200°C/400°F/Gas 6. Put the pasta in a large saucepan of boiling, salted water and cook for about 10 minutes, until just tender.

Meanwhile, in a large frying pan, heat the olive oil and gently fry the vegetables until beginning to soften. Add the garlic, tomato purée and tomatoes and stir well together. Add the thyme and oregano, season generously with salt and pepper, and simmer for 5 minutes.

Drain the cooked pasta and add the tomato mixture. Pour the mixture into a deep, oven-proof dish. Beat the eggs into the yoghurt and pour over the pasta.

Bake in the oven for about 15 minutes, until the yoghurt has set and formed a light golden crust. Serve hot.

PASTA AND NOODLES

As an Italian invention, it makes sense, of course, to drink Italian wine with pasta. What's it to be, though? Red or white? Still or sparkling? A light Valpolicella or thumping Barolo? After all, Italy makes every style of wine imaginable. It doesn't necessarily have to be Italian, however…hmm, I think we're back to square one!

Michael's delicious recipes inspire the answer: it's the flavour of the sauce that determines the best match. Choose a dryish, lively white or gentle, fruity red to go with the lighter dishes, switching to a rugged, heftier red for the stronger dishes.

Oaked Chardonnay from New Zealand, Australia or California is a dream with the *Tagliatelle with Peas and Smoked Salmon* (see p. 138). *Stir-fry Vegetable Noodles* (see p. 144) call for dry, nutty, breezy whites like Frascati or Soave. Michael's *Macaroni Pastitsio* (see p. 141) needs a crisp Italian white like the almondy-peachy Pinot Grigio or Bianco di Custoza. Alternatively, try a light, rustic Italian red – Bardolino or Rosso Cònero.

Michael's *Crispy Noodles with Crab Foo Yung* (see p. 137) is something else, though, and calls for a slightly stronger taste. Eggs are not the easiest ingredient to match with wine but, in this reicpe, it's the flavour of the crab and the sweet influence of the soy sauce that needs to be considered. Best bets include a slightly off-dry New World Riesling or Verdelho, and light reds, especially those made from Gamay, also match surprisingly well. These wines would also be super with the Three-layer Noodles with Prawns.

As for Pasta Shells with Blue Cheese Sauce…this sauce…! It shouts for something white and something sweet and racy such as German Kabinett or Spätlese – dry whites and reds won't work.

Bolognese provides a chance to test out sturdy red with swooping, peppery fruit and character – good, earthy, woodland-fruity Chianti (stretch to a Classico if you can), Crozes-Hermitage or Australian Shiraz.

Cooked Cheese

There are hundreds of pasta recipes that use cheese as an ingredient – but beware! Tannins in young red wine taste harsh with seriously cheesy dishes. Opt for a mature red from Spain or Southern Italy where tannin is less marked.

Onions
CRAFTY INGREDIENT

Quick Bolognese

Bolognese sauce is one of the great mistreated dishes of the world. Properly made in Bologna, it is rich and creamy and, although it normally needs to be simmered for a long time, some ingredients available today are able to produce a very similar sauce taking much less trouble and time. Although it's traditionally served with spaghetti, I quite like this sauce with the shorter, chunkier pastas, such as macaroni elbows, which seem to soak it up better. Suit yourself as to your choice of pasta.

time

25 mins

DRIED FRIED ONIONS

● These are sold in airtight plastic containers to retain the crispness that's needed when you're using them to sprinkle over South-East Asian dishes, which is one of their primary uses.

● They're excellent added to soups and stews and are a particularly quick way of making curry, as the slow frying of the onions normally required can be avoided by using the dried fried variety.

● Although they're pretty pungent, they also make a nice pre-dinner snack with drinks.

Serves 4

2 tablespoons olive oil
500 g (18 oz) minced beef
500 ml (17 fl oz) bottled fresh Italian tomato sauce
75 g (3 oz) dried fried onions
1 teaspoon garlic purée
salt and freshly ground black pepper
450 g (1 lb) spaghetti or macaroni elbows
120 ml (4 fl oz) double cream
1 teaspoon fresh or frozen basil
1 teaspoon fresh or frozen oregano
freshly grated Parmesan cheese, to serve

Heat 1 tablespoon olive oil in a heavy-based frying pan, add the minced beef and fry, stirring occasionally, until well browned. Add the tomato sauce, dried fried onions, and garlic, then stir together. Season generously with salt and pepper and simmer for 10–15 minutes.

Meanwhile, cook the pasta in a large saucepan of boiling, salted water for 10 minutes, then drain. Stir in the remaining olive oil to stop the pasta sticking, then turn into a large, warmed serving bowl.

Stir the cream into the sauce and add the basil and oregano. Pour into the centre of the pasta and serve with Parmesan cheese to sprinkle over each portion.

PASTA AND NOODLES

Stir-fry Vegetable Noodles

With the popularity of Far Eastern food, particularly stir-fries, a whole range of ingredients and products is now available to help create these dishes. A bowl of soup and some fruit afterwards turns this into a very quick and easy meal.

time

15 mins

Serves 4

250g (9 oz) packet Chinese-style noodles
salt
6 tablespoons cooking oil
350 g (12 oz) packet ready prepared stir-fry vegetables
350 g (12 oz) bean sprouts
2 eggs
85 ml (3 fl oz) soy sauce
I teaspoon garlic purée
I teaspoon ginger purée

Put the Chinese noodles into a saucepan of boiling water with a pinch of salt and a drop of oil and cook for 4 minutes. Drain and set aside. Meanwhile, rinse the stir-fry vegetables and bean sprouts and mix together.

Break the eggs into a bowl, add I tablespoon soy sauce and beat well together. Heat I tablespoon oil in a large frying pan, add the eggs and make a thin omelette, turning it over with a spatula or fish slice to cook gently on both sides.

Meanwhile, heat a wok or large frying pan, and add the remaining oil and the vegetables. Add the garlic and ginger purées and stir-fry over a high heat for a minute. Pour the remaining soy sauce around the edge of the pan, allowing it to sizzle its way down to the centre. Stir and toss for another 2–3 minutes. Remove two-thirds of the vegetables. Add the noodles to the remaining vegetables and toss together.

Pile the noodles on to a warmed serving plate and top with the stir-fried vegetables. Roll up the omelette, when it is cool enough to handle, and slice into 5 mm (¼ inch) ribbons. Use to garnish the dish before serving.

STIR-FRY VEGETABLE PACKETS

● Ready prepared stir-fry vegetable packets come in all styles and flavours. I tend to choose those that only contain vegetables, as I prefer my own style of seasoning. It's also best to make sure that the vegetables have been cut evenly and the same size because then they cook quickly and at the same speed. Another secret is to look for packets containing vegetables which require the same cooking time. Carrots, for example, when being stir-fried, take about 4 minutes longer than bean sprouts to cook. Having said all that, they're a great convenience and a terrific bonus.

● They also make an interesting salad, especially with an oriental dressing made by blending I teaspoon sugar, 2 tablespoons cider vinegar or white wine vinegar, and the same of soy sauce, 25 g (1 oz) peanut butter and 120 ml (4 fl oz) water in a liquidizer until smooth.

Three-layer Noodles with Prawns

Kenneth Lo, the master of Chinese cooking, taught me this very simple recipe, elegant in presentation and interesting in texture. Be careful how long you cook the prawns. They're delicious and succulent after a minute but Indian rubber after three or four minutes.

time

25 mins

● Bamboo shoots are an ingredient that has not yet arrived in any fresh form in Britain. They are exactly what they say – the trimmed and boiled shoots of large bamboo poles.

● Bamboo shoots are used in a range of different Chinese dishes. In addition to stir-fries, they are included in braised dishes and slow-cooked casseroles, usually flavoured with soy sauce and spices such as star anise. They are, however, very pleasant used in Western dishes where their crunchiness adds texture, even though their bland flavour is not very significant.

● Salads with a soft texture benefit greatly from them, cut into strips, matchsticks or cubes, and they add an interesting texture to soup.

Serves 4

250 g (9 oz) Chinese-style egg noodles
salt
2 tablespoons vegetable oil
I teaspoon garlic purée
I teaspoon ginger purée
I bunch spring onions, cut into 5 cm (2 inch) lengths
I red pepper, finely sliced
225 g (8 oz) can bamboo shoots, cut into matchsticks
2 tablespoons soy sauce
350 g (12 oz) cooked tiger prawns
175 g (6 oz) button mushrooms, halved
225 g (8 oz) can Italian chopped tomatoes
2 tablespoons black bean sauce

Put the noodles into a large saucepan of boiling, salted water with a drop of oil and boil for 3–4 minutes. Drain and set aside.

In a wok or large frying pan, heat the oil, then add the garlic, ginger, spring onions, red pepper and bamboo shoots and stir-fry over a high heat for 3–4 minutes until the vegetables are just softened. Add the soy sauce and the prawns and stir-fry for I minute only. Remove the prawns and two-thirds of the vegetables from the pan. Add the noodles to the remaining vegetables in the pan and stir-fry for another 2–3 minutes.

In a separate pan, put the mushrooms, chopped tomatoes and black bean sauce and bring gently to the boil, stirring.

To serve, pile the noodles on to a warmed serving dish, making a slight nest in the middle. Put the prawn and vegetable mixture in the centre and top with the tomato and mushroom sauce. Serve hot.

PASTA AND NOODLES

145

DESSERTS

FRUIT

If eggs are the ultimate quick savoury food, fruit has to be the obvious one in the field of puddings and desserts. However, it's worth thinking about the issue of ripeness. Most fruit we buy in greengrocers or supermarkets is picked green or under-ripe (in some cases, such as bananas, extremely under-ripe) and then ripened or matured on its way to us or in special ripening warehouses. Some supermarkets have developed the rather unpleasant habit of assuming we'll do this for them, thus saving them warehousing costs and storage problems, particularly in the case of bananas. The same thing applies to melons, which are often sold when they are so under-ripe that they have none of their natural fragrance. It's worth learning how to judge fruit and, to start with melons, the trick is to find the non-stalk end and see if it has a slight give to it. Also smell it. If it smells sweet then it's going to be ripe inside. You can't really tell with citrus fruit, except that if it's green it's not likely to have all its natural sweetness, but with pears you *can* tell. Gently feel at the base of the stalk to see whether or not there's any give. If there isn't, then they're not ready to eat, although they may ripen in your fruit bowl because pears ripen extremely quickly. With apples it's best to buy in season: English apples through the autumn and winter; and then apples from the southern hemisphere through the spring and summer when it is effectively *their* autumn and winter.

Fruit also makes the most wonderful puddings and desserts and I've included a number of different ones here, all with a surprising little twist to them. Like vegetables, fruit is now increasingly coming ready prepared. Some of the exotics, like pineapple and mangoes, are available ready peeled and sectioned. These are not only good to eat on their own but also very useful for making dishes such as fruit salads.

Apple Juice

Applejacks

These very simple, rustic pancakes are made in France, Canada and in Kent, all places where apples grow extremely well. They can be eaten either as a pudding or in a savoury form with grilled sausages and other similar meats. In this, they resemble American pancakes which are often eaten with what we would call a full English breakfast as well as a dessert. Applejacks, however, are very superior to American pancakes. It's almost impossible to make enough of them so you may want to make sure that the cook's portion is reserved before they all disappear.

time

25 mins

CLOUDY APPLE JUICE

● This is one of the most wonderful recent arrivals on the supermarket scene. It's fresh pressed apple juice which has not been dried, frozen or reconstituted in any way. It's also not been filtered too thoroughly so it has a thick, cloudy appearance and a delicious fresh flavour.

● Of necessity, it's always British produced and you may even find one company producing a variety of flavours, such as Coxes, Bramleys or Russets. Delicious to drink on their own, they also make splendid punches, or mulled drinks heated with a couple of cinnamon sticks, a spoonful of honey and a pinch of cloves.

● This sort of apple juice is also excellent as the basis of a sauce for fish or chicken, adding a slight sweet and sour taste. It can be used in batters and adds a lovely extra flavour to cakes.

Makes about 20

225 g (8 oz) eating apples, cored but not peeled
300 ml (10 fl oz) fresh pressed cloudy apple juice
225 g (8 oz) self-raising flour
2 eggs, beaten
2 teaspoons cooking oil, plus extra for greasing
apricot jam and whipped double cream, to serve

Grate the apples and quickly put them into a little of the apple juice so that they do not turn brown. Whisk in the flour and eggs, add the 2 teaspoons oil and the remaining apple juice, then whisk again. The batter should be like thin cream. If not, add a little more flour or apple juice as appropriate. Put in the fridge for 10–15 minutes, until slightly thick.

Heat a large, heavy-based frying pan and brush lightly with oil. Stir the batter to distribute the apple pieces, then place tablespoonfuls of the mixture, at intervals, around the pan, allowing room for spreading. Cook for about 1½ minutes until bubbles on the top start to burst. Turn them over carefully and continue to cook for another 1½–2 minutes, until golden brown. Remove from the pan and continue until all the batter is finished, greasing the pan every two or three times.

Serve hot, with a dollop of apricot jam and whipped cream.

FRUIT

How to read a Wine Label

FRENCH WINE

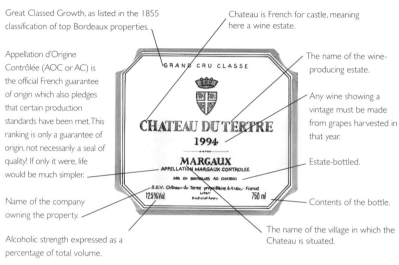

Great Classed Growth, as listed in the 1855 classification of top Bordeaux properties.

Chateau is French for castle, meaning here a wine estate.

Appellation d'Origine Contrôlée (AOC or AC) is the official French guarantee of origin which also pledges that certain production standards have been met. This ranking is only a guarantee of origin, not necessarily a seal of quality! If only it were, life would be much simpler.

The name of the wine-producing estate.

Any wine showing a vintage must be made from grapes harvested in that year.

Name of the company owning the property.

Estate-bottled.

Alcoholic strength expressed as a percentage of total volume.

Contents of the bottle.

The name of the village in which the Chateau is situated.

GERMAN WINE

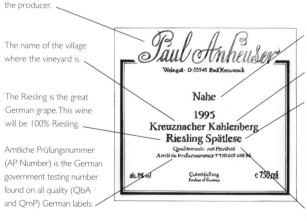

Name and address of the producer.

Name of the region of origin.

The name of the village where the vineyard is.

Name of the vineyard.

The Riesling is the great German grape. This wine will be 100% Riesling.

Top quality German wines are progressively classified by sweetness and richness as: Kabinett (the lightest, driest style), Spätlese, Auslese, Beerenauslese, Eiswein and Trockenbeerenauslese.

Amtliche Prüfungsnummer (AP Number) is the German government testing number found on all quality (QbA and QmP) German labels.

Qualitätswein mit Prädikat (QmP) best quality, naturally ripe, German wine with distinction.

ITALIAN WINE

Name of the producer.

Name of the region. Classico generally means the best-sited vineyards in the heart of the region.

It means the wine has had longer ageing and usually only the best wines are selected for this.

Wine name, in this case a top selection of their Chianti Classico.

Denominazione di Origine Controllata (DOC) is the official Italian classification similar to France's Appellation Contrôlée. Top wines are now awarded the ranking of DOCG – Denominazione di Origine Controllata e Garantita. Later vintages of this wine would be DOCG.

SPANISH WINE

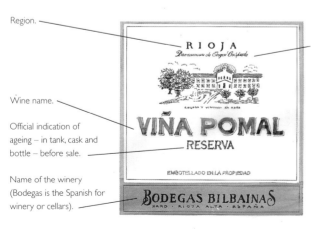

Region.

Wine name.

Official indication of ageing – in tank, cask and bottle – before sale.

Name of the winery (Bodegas is the Spanish for winery or cellars).

Denominacion de Origen (DO) is the official Spanish guarantee of origin and minimum production standards. The best wine regions are classified as Denominación de Origen Calificada (DOC).

OTHER USEFUL LABEL LORE

Bereich. German viticultural district surrounding a village. Bereich Nierstein, for example, is the district around Nierstein, but the quality is rarely thrilling.

Bin Number. Found on Australian wine labels, identifying a particular batch of wine.

Blanc de Blancs/Noirs. White wine made solely from white/black grapes.

Blush. Very pale rosé.

Brut/Sec/Secco/Trocken. Phrases meaning bone-dry.

Cava. Spanish sparkling wine made by the Champagne method.

Claret. Generic English word for red Bordeaux wines.

Co-operative. Winery jointly belonging to a number of small producers who pool costs and expertise.

Côte(s) and Coteau(x). French terms describing wines from higher, better ground - wine from Côtes de X is usually better than simple X.

Crianza. Spanish term to describe the youngest category of aged wine.

Cuvée. Contents of a vat; a blend; or a special batch of wine.

Demi-sec. Literally meaning half dry but in practice tastes semi-sweet.

Domaine. Wine-producing property or estate.

Espumoso/Sekt/Spumante. Spanish/German/Italian for sparkling wine.

Garrafeira. Top Portuguese wine.

Négociant. French term for a dealer who buys wines from various growers, then blends, matures and bottles them before selling under his own label.

Qualitätswein Bestimmter Anbaugebiete (QbA). Literally means quality wine from a specified region, the second highest category of German wine, which must meet certain minimum standards.

Quinta. Portuguese estate.

Supérieure/Superiore. Refers to French/Italian wines with a higher alcohol content. It doesn't follow that they taste superior!

Sur Lie. Lees are the yeast residues remaining in the cask after fermentation. Sur lie wines are bottled directly from the lees without racking, giving added freshness and creaminess.

Vin Délimité de Qualité Supérieure (VDQS). The second highest official quality category of French wine.

Vin de Pays. Country wine, the third official classification of French wines.

● It's possible to buy very
good-quality apple purée in
large jars (the small jars are
ideal for babies) with a little bit
of texture left in the apple.
Look for apple purées which
announce the fact that they're
made from Bramleys, if possible,
as they have the best flavour
and texture of all cooking
apples. Search for jars that have
no added ingredients except
perhaps a pinch of sugar.
● Apple purée makes all kinds
of dishes, including the filling
for a pie. It's also excellent
with rich roasted meats, such
as goose; mixed with a little
sugar and beaten egg to make
Apple Snow; and in dishes such
as trifles.

Brown Betty

Brown Betty is a rather countrified name given to an American version of a fruit cobbler. The brown colour comes from the sugar and the bread that was traditionally used to top it. It's a lovely rustic, autumn and winter dish that makes the best use of our wonderfully flavoured apples and apple purées. Although the Americans aren't particularly fond of it, I think custard, real or even from a packet, is terrific with this. Do try some of the new fresh custards that are available in the supermarkets' chilled cabinets.

time

15 mins

Serves 4

450 g (1 lb) apple purée (preferably Bramley)
100 g (4 oz) soft brown Barbados sugar
½ teaspoon ground cloves
½ teaspoon ground allspice
6 slices of brown or wholemeal bread
50 g (2 oz) butter

Pre-heat the grill. Put the apple purée, which can still have some chunks in it, into a saucepan. Add 50 g (2 oz) of the sugar and all the spices and bring slowly to boiling point, stirring until the sugar has dissolved. Pour into a pie dish or flameproof dish that will fit under the grill. Cut the bread slices into triangles and spread with the butter. Arrange in an overlapping pattern on top of the apple purée, butter side up, and sprinkle over the remaining sugar.

Place under the hot grill for about 5 minutes, until the bread is toasted and the butter and sugar mixture has melted together. Leave to cool for 1–2 minutes before serving and be careful when eating, as this is one of the hottest dishes I know.

FRUIT

Apple Purée
CRAFTY INGREDIENT

Blackberry Cobbler

Cobblers are dishes that are topped with bread or a close relative. Originally they were called cobblers because cobblers used to prepare soles and heels and lay them out in overlapping patterns on their work benches. Bread, when sliced and laid in a similar pattern on top of stews or fruit purées, gave the same impression and so the name was born. On this occasion I'm using sweet bread to go with a sweet ingredient. If fresh blackberries are in season do use them; otherwise frozen ones are great and canned ones passable. Lots of thick cream or yoghurt goes really well with this dish.

time

30 mins

Serves 6

450 g (1 lb), fresh or frozen blackberries or four 420 g (14 oz)
    cans blackberries in juice
1–3 tablespoons caster sugar
4 brioche buns
50 g (2 oz) butter

Pre-heat the oven to 200°C/400°F/Gas 6. If using fresh or frozen blackberries, put them in a saucepan with the sugar, according to taste, and 100 ml (3½ fl oz) water. Bring slowly to the boil and simmer for 5–10 minutes until just soft. If using canned blackberries, drain, reserving the juice. Pour the cooked blackberries and their juice or the canned blackberries and 4 tablespoons of the reserved juice into a gratin dish or pie dish, about 10 cm (4 inches) deep.

Cut each brioche bun into three, 1 cm (½ inch) thick slices and spread generously with butter. Place the slices in an overlapping pattern, butter side up, over the blackberries and sprinkle with 1 teaspoon, no more, of caster sugar.

Bake in the oven for about 20 minutes, until the brioche is golden and the blackberries bubbling.

BRIOCHE

● Brioche is a yeast-risen, French, sweet bread. It can be bought as loaves or buns. It toasts well and is used in expensive restaurants to serve with foie gras or special pâtés.
● It makes a spectacular Bread and Butter Pudding and is great dipped in *café au lait* for breakfast, as they do in Paris.

Brioche
CRAFTY INGREDIENT

Poached Peaches in Elderflower Syrup

A dish for high summer when peaches are plentiful and you can bear cooking them rather than just eating them fresh. This is a very elegant pudding which can be served in the kind of champagne glass that used to appear in 1950s films – flat, shallow and rather like a curved saucer on a stem. It's equally good in ordinary china bowls, as the delicate peach flesh and the fragrant elderflower flavours make a marvellous combination.

time

30 mins

Serves 4

4 large ripe peaches, preferably white-fleshed
50 g (2 oz) caster sugar
75 ml (3 fl oz) elderflower syrup

Bring a large saucepan of water to the boil, then dip the peaches in for 40 seconds – 1 minute. Remove and, when cool enough to handle, slip off the skins. If you wish, halve the peaches and remove the stones or, for a more spectacular presentation, remove the stone from the base, leaving the peach as whole as possible.

Put the sugar, elderflower syrup and 750 ml (1¼ pints) water in a non-stick saucepan. Add the peaches, bring to simmering point and simmer, covered, for 5 minutes if they have been halved or 8–10 minutes if they're still whole, turning every 2–3 minutes until evenly heated but still firm.

Remove the peaches from the pan, put in a serving dish and pour over the syrup. Leave to cool a little, then serve warm. They can also be kept in the fridge for up to 24 hours and served cold.

ELDERFLOWER SYRUP

● Elderflower syrup is a traditional country store cupboard product which is made by steeping elderflowers in water, adding sugar and boiling the mixture down for bottling. A number of different firms are producing elderflower syrup of very good quality these days in bottles. It always needs diluting, as it's very powerfully flavoured.

● A couple of teaspoonfuls will flavour fizzy water and ice in a tall glass for a most delicious muscat-flavoured summer drink.

● It's also very good added to the syrup for fruit salads and, surprisingly enough, as a sparingly used ingredient in cream sauce for salmon.

FRUIT

● Although blended honey is widely available, quite delicious and very cheap, it's worth looking for individually flavoured honeys, such as clove, or thyme which is dark, powerful and fragrant, or wild flower honey.

● When making honey, bees extract the nectar from specific kinds of flowers and so impart some of the flavour into the honey. Whilst they're more expensive, they make delicious additions to specific dishes such as Welsh Lamb Baked with Honey or Honey and Ginger Cake. Flavoured honeys are also delicious just eaten on hot, buttered toast.

Microwaved Apples

Baked apples are a great British tradition and this is a very simple variation. You can of course cook this dish in a conventional oven if you wish but it takes about twice as long. My favourite way of serving this is with just a little thin, not double, cream, which mixes wonderfully with the honey juices. Do, by the way, use eating apples for this recipe; cooking apples are much too large and cook in quite a different way. They also don't seem to have the same fragrance.

time

20 mins

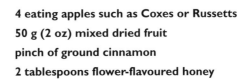

Serves 4

4 eating apples such as Coxes or Russetts
50 g (2 oz) mixed dried fruit
pinch of ground cinnamon
2 tablespoons flower-flavoured honey

Using the point of a sharp knife, make a shallow cut around the middle of each apple. (This stops the skin splitting any further when you bake them.) Core the apples, leaving a small piece in the base to prevent all the filling falling out. Mix together the dried fruit and cinnamon and use to stuff the apples. Place the apples in a microwave-proof dish and pour the honey over the top, making sure some of it goes inside the apples. Add 250 ml (8 fl oz) water. Place inside the microwave and cook on HIGH/100% power for 10–15 minutes, depending on the power and instructions of your microwave, until soft. Serve each apple with spoonfuls of the juices.

FRUIT

Honey
CRAFTY INGREDIENT

 WINE # Champagne and Sparkling Wines

'I drink it when I'm happy and when I'm sad. Sometimes I drink it when I'm alone. When I have company I consider it obligatory. I trifle with it if I'm not hungry and drink it when I am. Otherwise I never touch it – unless I'm thirsty.'

Madame Bollinger

It's the zenith of any-day, any-time sippers. Celebrations have to have it. It doesn't always matter what it is, just as long as it's there. Yes, this is that most charming, irresistible, suavely graceful wine – fizz.

For most of us Champagne is *the* great treat – but why is it so special and what do we crack open instead if the budget is stretched? Traditionalists argue that Champagne's breeding comes from the region's chalky soil. Others say it's all to do with the balance of grape varieties – Pinot Noir, Chardonnay and Pinot Meunier. In reality, though, it's a magical marriage of both, coupled with the distinctive way in which Champagne is made.

Champagne's delightful, tongue-tingling frothiness comes from tiny bubbles. The smaller the bubble, the better the quality. Tiny bubbles can only be created in the bottle itself, by the Champagne Method – some yeast and sugar is added to ordinary wine which makes it re-ferment. As the bottle is tightly corked, carbon dioxide, a natural by-product, is unable to escape – hence the sparkle.

Budget Options

The Champagne method of production has been imitated all around the globe, so as long as you can distinguish between a genuine lookalike and over-priced fizzy dross, it is possible to drink Champagne-quality at half the price. Simply shop for wines made by the Champagne method (labelled Méthode Traditionelle or words to that effect).

Apart from a host of superbly-priced, supple, stylish versions from the New World, especially those made by limbs of the Champagne houses, all French Appellation Contrôlée sparkling wines must be made in this way, as is Cava, Spain's popular answer to Champagne.

PREPARED PINEAPPLE

● This is perhaps one of the most astonishing prepared fruits, as it appears not only to last well and be effortless to use but also tastes better than most fresh pineapples you prepare yourself. This may be because the pineapples are prepared at the point when they reach their maximum ripeness rather than being shipped green. Either way, it's excellent simply eaten as a fruit or used as an ingredient in a dish such as crumble.

● It's also perfect, in moderate quantities, used in sweet and sour Chinese dishes, cut into cubes and put on skewers with large tiger prawns or large chunks of Gruyère cheese before grilling.

Quick Fruit Salad

Fruit salads are always welcome and always delicious, especially if two or three simple rules are followed. Never use more than four fruits, make sure the fruit is cut up into similar-size pieces, make sure you have some liquid that binds it, and don't be tempted to use canned fruit. This recipe makes use of many of the prepared ingredients that are available these days. You can, of course, use different fruits depending on what you find in the shops. The mixture of colour and texture is the key to a successful fruit salad.

time

30 mins

Serves 4

1 prepared fresh pineapple in juice
2 seedless clementines or small oranges
1 large or 2 small eating apples
2 bananas
single cream, to serve (optional)

Pour the pineapple juice into a serving bowl. Cut the pineapple into 1 cm (½ inch) dice and add to the bowl. Peel the clementines or oranges and divide into segments. Core the apple, but do not peel, cut into wedges and then into 1 cm (½ inch) slices. Add to the bowl with the clementine segments. Slice the bananas into the bowl, then stir together. Put into the coldest part of the fridge for about 20 minutes to chill before serving. Serve with cream, if wished.

FRUIT

Pineapple
CRAFTY INGREDIENT

Individual Apricot Crumbles

Crumbles are that most British of puddings, usually made with our traditional fruits such as apples or gooseberries, but in fact they work well with more exotic ingredients. Here, apricots in a couple of different forms are combined with an unusual and extremely simple topping. It's the sort of thing you can actually put together in five minutes while making sure that the rest of the meal's under control. And it's a pudding much appreciated as virtually everyobody loves the flavour of apricots.

time

30 mins

Serves 4

175 g (6 oz) no-soak dried apricots
2 tablespoons apricot conserve
75 g (3 oz) apricot muesli

Pre-heat the oven to 200°C/400°F/Gas 6.

Put the apricots into a non-stick saucepan with 150 ml (5 fl oz) water. Bring to the boil, then simmer for 10 minutes, until softened. Put in a food processor and blend until smooth, then blend in the apricot conserve.

Pour the mixture into individual soufflé or ramekin dishes and sprinkle over the muesli, to cover completely. Place on a baking tray and bake in the oven for 15 minutes, until the topping has blended with the top layer of the filling and is slightly browned. Serve with custard or cream.

MUESLI

● Muesli comes in all kinds of flavours, from the extremely pure, simple, virtually nothing added kind, to honey-coated and nut-clustered. One to look out for, for this dish, is apricot and almond cluster.

● Apart from making delicious breakfast cereals, they're also wonderful stirred into home-made ice-cream before you freeze it, as an extra and unexpected ingredient in a home-made biscuit mixture, and, without the milk, as a crunchy high fibre snack.

Muesli

CRAFTY INGREDIENT

I hardly dare include some of these recipes because they are so crafty as to be outrageous. You buy a first-class ice-cream (more about that in a moment), then make an almost instantaneous topping which adds luxury, flavour and excitement to what may already be great ice-cream. Some of these are very traditional toppings brought up to date and others, I have to confess, are frankly a chocaholic's indulgence.

As far as the ice-cream is concerned, there is a really wide range of very good ice-cream now available in Britain. The flavours are often extraordinary, and sometimes magnificent, but for home use I tend to go for good old-fashioned vanilla, strawberry or chocolate because they work so well with toppings.

When you're shopping for ice-cream, don't necessarily assume that a fancy label equals good ice-cream. Look for cream and eggs in the ingredients and avoid those containing hydrogenated vegetable fat. Also be aware that ice-cream can be very aerated, meaning that the real ingredients may only make up half the quantity because of the volume of air. Therefore, sometimes a fairly large tub of ice-cream may seem better value than a smaller one but, in fact, may contain less weight. It's always worth checking.

One last hint: if you're serving ice-cream and you've been keeping it in the freezer, leave it in the fridge for half an hour before you scoop and serve it. This will soften it enough to be easy to serve and to eat but it won't lose any of its texture.

Raspberry Coulis

If you've ever seen a 'stop me and buy one' ice-cream van putting a dark red syrupy mixture on top of an ice-cream cone, you've seen the remnants of a great tradition – raspberry-flavoured sauces used on ice-cream. The French word, coulis, is one that's more familiar to modern chefs, but in fact this form of flavouring is very British and goes back a long way. It was traditionally made with vinegar and, indeed, some forms of it were simply a sweetened raspberry-flavoured vinegar. This version is rather richer than that and combines the old flavourings with generous amounts of fruit

time

10 mins

Serves 4

250 g (9 oz) fresh raspberries
2 tablespoons icing sugar
2 teaspoons balsamic vinegar
vanilla ice-cream, to serve

Put the raspberries in a small saucepan with 85 ml (3 fl oz) water and simmer gently for about 5 minutes, until softened. Pour into a food processor and blend until smooth. Push through a sieve, into a bowl, to remove the seeds, then stir in the sugar and balsamic vinegar. Serve poured over vanilla ice-cream.

BALSAMIC VINEGAR

● This is produced in and around the town of Modena in Italy. It almost vanished at the beginning of the century and was brought back when it was discovered that its rich, dark flavours made a wonderful difference to a whole range of dishes. A small bottle goes a long way. Make sure you get the authentic product, as there are a lot of cheap copies around which are not worth buying.

● A teaspoon or two added to a salad dressing gives a lovely depth and slightly sweet and sour flavour.

● Surprising though it sounds, it's delicious dribbled in small quantities over strawberries with a little sugar added (no cream please!).

● I like to add a spoonful of it to Pesto Sauce before mixing it with hot pasta.

Balsamic Vinegar
CRAFTY INGREDIENT

Cheat's Chocolate Sauce

It is an outrageous proposition to put this sauce over good-quality ice-cream and it should only be done if you have no concern for calories. This sauce is, however, very delicious. I hardly feel able to recommend it but, as it's so easy and effortless to make, you might care to make up your own mind. Nevertheless, however good the sauce, the better the quality of ice-cream the better the dish will taste. The availability of really excellent ice-creams, made from eggs and cream and fresh milk, is really very encouraging.

time

5 mins

Serves 4

two 100g (4oz) Mars® bars
120 ml (4 fl oz) milk
ice-cream, to serve
1 chocolate flake bar, to serve

Cut the Mars® bars into 1 cm (½ inch) slices. Pour the milk into a non-stick saucepan, add the Mars® bar slices and heat gently, stirring until a thick caramel sauce is formed. (Do not let the mixture boil.) Pour over servings of ice-cream. Crumble the flake bar over the top and serve immediately.

MARS® BARS

● I'm not sure that this ingredient needs any further introduction except that, in addition to being eaten in the normal way and turned into ice-cream sauce, my family has for many years, placed it in the freezer for an hour before slicing it very thinly. It is then eaten as a form of Mars® bar ice-cream (before they began production anyway).

ICE-CREAM TOPPINGS

● These come in a variety of forms these days. These include roasted and salted, which you can recognize from the open shells; roasted and unsalted, which are ideal for this recipe; and shelled, which are green and pink in colour.

● Traditionally, they are used as a flavouring for ice-cream although this requires a certain amount of work on the grinding front.

● They're delicious salted and shelled, or mixed with rice, onions and a little allspice to make a stuffing for small birds such as quail or poussin.

● Quick-fried in a little oil, after removing their shells, they're a good alternative to pine nuts on salads. Ground up or finely chopped, they make a splendid addition to nut pastries and tarts such as Baklava.

Butterscotch Pistachio Sauce

We tend to think of pistachios as a savoury nut, particularly as, in this country, we usually come across the salted variety, but in the nineteenth century they were almost always used in sweet dishes. Pistachio ice-cream is one example and in the Middle East they are baked in many pastries and often flavoured with honey or other similar sweet ingredients. This is a very simple sauce which has a fudgy flavour with a crispness and crunchiness coming from the nuts. Be careful not to buy salted pistachios.

time

10 mins

Serves 4

100 g (4 oz) butter
100 g (4 oz) runny honey
50 g (2 oz) shelled, toasted and roughly chopped pistachio nuts
ice-cream, to serve

Put the butter and honey into a small saucepan and gently heat, stirring occasionally, until the butter has melted. Bring to the boil and simmer for 5 minutes, then stir thoroughly and stir in the pistachio nuts. Allow to cool slightly before serving, poured over ice-cream.

Pistachio Nuts
CRAFTY INGREDIENT

ICE-CREAM TOPPINGS

Hot Banana Toffee

This ice-cream topping comes from the Southern States of America where it's often served at Sunday brunch, to end the very substantial meals that pass for a light repast there.. It's interesting that it includes some of the traditional products of the Southern States, as well as the wonderful molasses flavour of dark brown sugar and bananas which were so much a part of the traditional cooking of the slaves.

time

5 mins

Serves 4

2 large, ripe bananas
50 g (2 oz) butter
100 g (4 oz) Barbados soft dark brown sugar
½ teaspoon ground cinnamon
½ teaspoon ground allspice
vanilla ice-cream, to serve

Peel the bananas, cut them in half lengthways and then cut across into two pieces. Put them in a frying pan (preferably non-stick, to help with the washing up rather than to affect the cooking). Add the butter and cook until heated through but not completely disintegrated. Sprinkle with the sugar, add the spices and stir quickly. Cook over a medium heat until the sugar and butter have melted together into a form of soft toffee. Spoon over vanilla ice-cream and serve immediately.

BARBADOS SUGAR

● The soft brown sugars (not Demerara which is another matter altogether) are the least refined of all sugars. Despite any publicity to the contrary, this doesn't significantly affect their nutritional value, as they contain no more fibre or vitamins than white sugar does, but it does affect their flavour.

● They bring a richness to all kinds of cakes and biscuits, fruit purées and sweet dishes. To many people they are the best sorts of sugars to put in black coffee.

ICE-CREAM TOPPINGS

Barbados Sugar
CRAFTY INGREDIENT

Thanks to memories of schooldays, the mention of milk puddings can produce a shudder. While I've had my share of tapioca, I was lucky that both my grandmother and mother produced wonderful milk puddings at home. A particularly fine Bread and Butter Pudding comes to mind. It's interesting that, while most modern British chefs have moved to the Mediterranean for their first two or three courses, it's usually back to British basics for their puddings. The fact is that milk and its derivatives – yoghurt, fromage frais, soft cheeses, creams and buttermilk – make the most wonderful bases for puddings.

The range can be a bit confusing and, apart from milk itself (which comes in everything from what used to be gold top, and is now called breakfast milk, to an almost totally skimmed version), there is so much else. The French version of cream is called crème fraîche and comes in whole and half-fat versions. Both are solid and firm in texture and therefore spoonable, though neither whips particularly well. Then there's fromage frais, which comes in an 8–10 per cent fat content and a zero fat variety. It also comes in a slightly drier German version called quark. Yoghurts (leaving aside the issue of organic versus non-organic) range from Greek yoghurt, which has been strained so it has about 10 per cent fat, to whole milk yoghurts, low fat yoghurts, solid set yoghurts, and drinking yoghurts which are exactly that, quite liquid and always flavoured with fruit. Drinking yoghurts are a great tradition from the Middle East, where both savoury and sweet varieties are enjoyed.

Finally, there are the more unexpected and obscure milk products such as cultured buttermilk and smetana, a thick, rich, sour cream product from Eastern Europe. They tend to be rather sharper than the flavours we're used to and are very good in cooking. They are the traditional additions to dishes such as Goulash and Borsch, the famous Russian Beetroot Soup. I like them, however, on pancakes, particularly if they contain some sweet and fruity jam such as red plum or golden apricot.

Almond and Pear Pudding

*Classic French cooking used to include a whole range of puddings based on
rice, which bore no resemblance at all to the British baked rice pudding.
Normally, the rice was cooked in advance and then mixed with a variety of
fruits and that's the technique I've used here. If fresh pears are in season
you can use those, but canned pears are excellent too. Look for varieties
canned in natural juice. Don't leave out the almonds, they make all the
difference to the texture of this very simple dish.*

time

15 mins

Serves 4

420 g (14½ oz) can ready made rice pudding
   (made with whole milk)
4 pear halves, skinned and poached for 10 minutes,
   or a 420 g (14 oz) can pears in juice
½ teaspoon cinnamon
50 g (2 oz) toasted almonds

Pre-heat the oven to 200°C/400°F/Gas 6.

Put the rice pudding into a non-stick saucepan and heat gently.
Meanwhile, slice the pears and arrange them in 4 individual ramekin
dishes, or 1 large 900 ml (1½ pint) soufflé dish, to cover the bottom.
Sprinkle over the cinnamon, pour over the rice pudding and sprinkle
over the almonds.

Bake in the oven for 10–15 minutes, until the whole dish is heated
through. Serve hot.

TOASTED ALMONDS

● It may seem a total
indulgence having someone
toast almond flakes for you.
But in fact, as far as I'm
concerned, it makes the
difference between using them
and not bothering. During a
busy week, toasted almond
flakes are a great boon.

● They're good on all sorts of
puddings but they're also
excellent on savoury dishes,
such as trout fillets fried in
butter with dill, or as an
addition to a dish of lightly
curried chicken and pilau rice.

MILK AND DAIRY

● These are available in all shapes and sizes of bottles. Some of the best are made in Britain, are organic and made with real fruit and no artificial flavours. It's worth looking out for the best-quality drinking yoghurt you can find. Strawberry, raspberry and apricot flavours are my favourites.

● As well as being useful for making desserts, they are also an excellent base for the kind of summer fruit soups that are so popular in Eastern Europe. Fresh fruit is sliced into sour cream or buttermilk and garnished with mint before being served in small cups at the end of a meal.

Frozen Yoghurt Dessert

This is a kind of low-fat alternative to ice-cream that can be made in a variety of flavours. I've suggested strawberry on this occasion but, depending on the drinking yoghurt flavour you buy, it's very much something you can vary. This crafty recipe greatly reduces the time required by making it in an ice-cream machine.

time

30 mins

Serves 4

100 g (4 oz) strawberries, hulled
15 g (½ oz) caster sugar
2 egg whites
1 litre (1¾ pints) strawberry drinking yoghurt

Chop the strawberries into small pieces and put in a bowl. Sprinkle with the caster sugar. Whisk the egg whites until stiff. Mix the drinking yoghurt with the strawberries and fold in the egg whites. Then pour into an ice-cream machine and freeze according to the manufacturer's instructions.

To keep, put into a plastic container, cover with a lid and store in the freezer.

Yoghurts
CRAFTY INGREDIENT

MILK AND DAIRY

Blueberry Fool

Fruit fools are really a British invention. Although similar dishes are made all over the world, no one else has quite captured the market in terms of variety and style. In this dish I'm recreating something I knew in my childhood where it was made with Welsh blueberries, which are known locally as whinberries. American blueberries, which are readily available (whereas whinberries need individual picking for a short two-week season in summer), are much larger and brighter in colour, though not necessarily stronger in flavour. They make a lovely purple fool which in this version is comparatively low in fat, as I'm using the wonderful trick of whipping yoghurt with cream to make a low-fat mixture that's just as thick as whipped cream.

time

30 mins

Serves 4

275 g (10 oz) fresh blueberries
50 g (2 oz) caster sugar
150 ml (5 fl oz) whipping cream
150 ml (5 fl oz) whole-milk yoghurt

Put the blueberries in a bowl and, using a spoon or fork, crush them until they yield their juice. Stir in 25 g (1 oz) of the sugar and leave for 10 minutes.

Meanwhile, whip the whipping cream until stiff. Add a spoonful of the yoghurt and a spoonful of the remaining sugar alternately, and continue to whip the cream until it is stiff again and all the yoghurt has been incorporated. Stir together the crushed blueberries and their juice, then stir into the cream mixture until fairly well mixed but leaving a slight marbled effect. Pour into 4 wine glasses or individual serving dishes and put in the fridge for about 15 minutes to set. (The fools can be kept in the fridge for 2–3 hours before serving.)

FRESH BLUEBERRIES

● Blueberries, along with many other berries and fresh fruits, are now being packaged for our convenience. They come almost exclusively in this form from North America and have a remarkably good 'shelf life'.

● Apart from being incorporated into fruit salads and fresh fruit dishes, to which they add colour and pungency, they're also used a lot for baking, particularly blueberry muffins and pancakes.

● Be careful with the juice, as, once it stains, it's seriously difficult to get out.

Blueberries
CRAFTY INGREDIENT

Crafty Strawberry Brûlée

Brûlées are dishes with a crunchy caramelized sugar coating. They're traditionally made by spreading sugar on top of the made dish and then heating it under the grill until the sugar melts and bubbles. This is all very fine but has a couple of drawbacks. One is that it's quite difficult to get right and, secondly, it can heat and spoil the ingredients underneath the sugar. I developed this crafty way of making a brûlée a couple of years ago, while looking for an easy alternative.

time

30 mins

Serves 4

225 g (8 oz) strawberries
I tablespoon plus 100 g (4 oz) caster sugar
300 ml (10 fl oz) 8 per cent fat fromage frais

Put the strawberries in a bowl and, using a fork, roughly crush. Gently stir in the I tablespoon of sugar. Put the fromage frais into a 600 ml (I pint) soufflé dish or serving dish. Beat it until smooth, then add the crushed strawberry mixture, swirling it to produce a marbled effect. Smooth the top down as flat as possible.

In a non-stick saucepan, put 50 ml (2 fl oz) water and 100 g (4 oz) sugar and bring gently to the boil, stirring with a wooden spoon, until the mixture starts to turn golden brown. (Watch carefully as this happens quickly.) Carefully but quickly pour the mixture, in a spiral pattern, over the strawberry mixture to form a caramel topping. It should spread together naturally to cover all the spaces. If not, melt a little more sugar and water together and use this to patch the gaps. Leave for I5 minutes to set, before serving. (Do not put in the fridge as the topping will go soft.) The pudding can be left at room temperature for up to 4 hours before serving.

FROMAGE FRAIS

● There are two main types of fromage frais – a French version with the name fromage frais and a German one sometimes known as quark. Quark tends to be a bit drier but otherwise they are very similar, ranging from zero to about 10 per cent fat content. While the no-fat varieties are very pleasant in their own right, when it comes to cooking or adding other ingredients the slightly higher fat varieties tend to be more desirable as they stay together better and have a slightly creamier taste.

● They are good in puddings and fools where cream would be used, delicious stirred into savoury soups, and as a topping for casseroles, particularly Hungarian dishes with paprika.

● They also make very delicious instant puddings with a little good-quality conserve or French jam stirred into them. Put into little pots and top with a few toasted almonds.

MILK AND DAIRY

Honey and Walnut Yoghurt

This combination is so popular that you can actually buy yoghurts with honey added but they're simply not in the same class as ones you make yourself. It takes a matter of moments to achieve, providing you've got the right ingredients. I strongly recommend that you try making this yourself. Although it's meant to be a pudding, it's also quite delicious at breakfast time, if you're moderate with the honey.

● This is a dark brown mountain honey from Greece, which is supplied by bees which seem to feed almost exclusively on the wild thyme plants in the mountains. It therefore has the richest herb scent of any honey I know, and is marvellous eaten on its own on bread or toast or hot buttered crumpets.

● You can use it in baking and cooking, substituting it for the same amount of sugar but leaving a little liquid out of the mixture as the honey contains water.

● It's also superb used to coat roast lamb halfway through its roasting in the traditional Welsh style, although they've never had such delicious honey as this in Wales. The herb flavour seems to blend particularly well with the savouriness of the meat.

time

30 mins

Serves 4

300ml (10 fl oz) Greek natural yoghurt
4 tablespoons hymettus honey
75g (3 oz) walnut halves

Pour the yoghurt into a bowl and stir until smooth. Drizzle in the honey from a spoon, stirring, to produce a marbled effect. Crush three-quarters of the walnut halves in your hands, or between 2 sheets of greaseproof paper using a rolling pin. Stir into the yoghurt mixture. Pour into 4 tall glasses to show the marbling effect and sprinkle the top with the remaining walnut halves. Allow to chill in the fridge for 20 minutes before serving.

Hymettus Honey
CRAFTY INGREDIENT

MILK AND DAIRY

RED GRAPES

Cabernet Sauvignon is the world's most famous, most travelled, red wine grape with an unstoppable personality. It's the bedrock of an astonishing number of 'Fine Wines' from California, Australia, Italy, Spain, Chile and Lebanon, but its most celebrated expression is released in Bordeaux's Médoc.

Top Cabernets need years to evolve, softening dark, masculine tannins into sweet, feminine blackberry-blackcurrant fruits mingled with a dry fragrance of cedarwood. Fear not, though, if the piggy bank's only half full; there's also a flood of attractive, punchy, mid-priced Cabernets.

Merlot lends its soothing hand to plenty of blends, playing chorus line to big-name, star-time grapes. In claret, for example, it's the unacknowledged twin to the famed Cabernet Sauvignon, fleshing out Cabernet's austere nature.

There is also a myriad of stand-alone showcase Merlots, in southern France, Italy, Eastern Europe and the Americas, offering voluptuous, plump, fruit-filled wonders bursting with rounded, slightly sweet, damson and coffee bean flavours.

Pinot Noir is the Holy Grail of red grapes that everyone wants to grow but can't because it's fussy, capricious and difficult to handle. At its finest, in Burgundy, it creates magical wines of elegance, complexity and finesse, teeming with lush, strawberry-raspberry flavours in youth, mellowing to a violet-scented, truffles-and-game style with maturity.

It seems unlikely that Burgundy will ever be truly emulated but, in the process of trying, winemakers worldwide are discovering that their own individual styles can be just as alluring.

Syrah is a fascinating, seductive and much underrated variety that is not taken seriously enough outside France's Rhône Valley and Australia (where it's Shiraz). This is surprising, as Syrah is so versatile, but South Africa and California are beginning to find this out.

No single description can ever really capture the Syrah taste. It achieves a unique fusion of rich spice, majestic structure and longevity, embracing opulent, intensely sweet, ripe, jammy, smoky, inky, raspberry-blueberry-blackcurrant-plum-elderberry-black cherry laden fruit with liquorice and chocolate in a concentrated, chewy style…phew!

WHITE GRAPES

Chardonnay is our favourite white grape. Winemakers adore it as it's child's play to grow. We drinkers love it, swilling down gallons of the stuff each year. Made simply, it's the canvas for the individual character of the region beneath a clean, nutty-edged, citrus, easy-going, dry style. However, fermented or aged in oak, it becomes a noble, fat beast, soaking up the oak's spice and cream flavours.

To many, white Burgundy is the quintessential Chardonnay – minerally, lissome, sophisticated, with just a whisper of buttery-oak flavours and built to last. New World Chardonnays are quite different – rich, oozing exuberant, vanilla-tinged, sunshine-ripe fruit. California boasts the biggest and burliest. Australian Chardonnay is sun-baked and fruit-driven. In New Zealand, it's lemony and packed with exotic tropical fruit.

Chilean Chardonnay should be nervier, almost perfumed, with a tangy twist and South Africa offers a style poised between the Old World and the New.

Rhine Riesling – and I mean Rhine, not Laski – rivals Chardonnay as the best white wine maker, especially in Germany where it makes superlative sweet wines. Fresh and flowery with slices-of-lime-and-lemon zest bite in infancy, it ages to lovely, classy, petrolly aromas and honey flavours that positively leap out of the glass.

Riesling has the potential to produce some of the finest whites in the world but it's hardly cultivated in Europe outside Germany, Austria and Alsace. It's widely grown in Australia, though, where it ripens more, giving silky-soft wines with lower acidity and baked apple flavours and New Zealand Riesling can also be brilliant.

Sauvignon Blanc is the Bramley to most other white grape's Golden Delicious — bracing, assertive, penetrating acidity is its signature. With some of the most pronounced aromas of all grapes (gooseberries, elderflower, freshly-mown grass, asparagus, cat's pee) it's uncompromising and unforgettable.

Sancerre, from France's Loire valley, is the rôle-model of the bone-dry style. Its green-gooseberry fruit and gunflint perfume has inspired wine-makers the world over, in Italy, Eastern Europe, South Africa, California, Australia and Chile but, above all, it excels in New Zealand where it takes on a pungent, herbaceous smoothness.

Sauvignon is also a crucial ingredient in the aristocratic sweet wines of Bordeaux's Sauternes and Barsac, where its acid grip balances cloying sweetness.

Muscat is the only variety that joyously and exultantly tastes of grapes themselves! Mind you, variety is the wrong word — there are over 200 types of Muscat in one big happy grape family! Some of them end up in our fruit bowls — only four are important in wine-making.

Muscat makes three distinct styles — the refreshing, delicately pale, hauntingly perfumed, dry versions from France, Italy and Hungary; the lusciously concentrated, marmalade flavoured, heady, fortified styles in France, Spain, Portugal, Australia and South Africa; last, but not least, gorgeously sweet and dazzling Italian fizz.

Sémillon, with its thin skin, is prone to Noble Rot — which doesn't sound particularly nice but, believe me, is one of the best things that can happen to certain grapes. This type of rot gives birth to some of the finest sweet wines in the world, most particularly Bordeaux's Sauternes and Barsac. Unrotted Sémillon is also used to make dry wines, either on its own or as part of a blend, with delicate, lemon-fresh flavours in youth, ageing into a glorious, richly-honeyed, nutty beast. The best dry styles come from France's Graves district, Australia, South Africa, California, New Zealand and Washington State.

● This is a dairy product that originates in Eastern Europe. It's quite thick and creamy and has the same pouring texture as double cream but is much, much lower in fat, being made from the residue of the milk after the fat has been removed for butter making.

● It has a slightly sourer flavour than yoghurt and sour cream but goes well with both savoury and sweet dishes.

● It's the correct ingredient to add to Goulash and goulash soups, rather than sour cream. It goes marvellously in Borsch, that dark, rich, red beetroot soup from Russia, but is also good as an alternative to cream on puddings and fresh fruit.

Strawberry and Banana Boffo

A wonderful name for a highly flavoured and exotic milkshake. This one is made with an unusual mixture of cultured buttermilk which adds a touch of sourness and even, dare I say it, adult appeal. I find that a glass of this goes down very well as the start to a Sunday brunch for the whole family.

time

5 mins

Serves 4

2 ripe bananas
225g (8 oz) strawberries, hulled
175 ml (6 fl oz) cultured buttermilk
600 ml (1 pint) semi-skimmed milk
1 tablespoon caster sugar, to taste

Peel the bananas and cut into 2.5 cm (1 inch) chunks. Halve the strawberries if they are very large.

Put the fruits in a food processor, add the buttermilk and the milk and blend thoroughly. Add the sugar, to taste, and blend again.

Serve in tall glasses with a straw, if wished.

Buttermilk

CRAFTY INGREDIENT

MILK AND DAIRY

Crafty Tiramisu

Literally, this means 'pick-me-up' and it's a fairly recently invented Italian pudding which seems to have caught on all over the world. This might be because of the degree of self-indulgence it involves – rich layers of chocolate, coffee-soaked biscuits, sweet Italian cream cheese and sometimes other goodies such as rum or brandy. This is a quick version which hangs on to most of the flavours but doesn't take quite so long to make.

time

20 mins

Serves 4

1 tablespoon good-quality instant coffee

75 g (3 oz) icing sugar

8–10 boudoir biscuits

350 g (12 oz) mascarpone cheese

2 eggs, separated

3 chocolate flake bars, crumbled,
   or 75 g (3 oz) milk chocolate, grated

Pour 150 ml (5 fl oz) boiling water over the coffee, add 2 teaspoons of the icing sugar and stir until dissolved. Put a layer of biscuits, sugar side up, in the base of a 600 ml (1 pint) soufflé dish or 4 small individual ramekin dishes. Pour over the coffee mixture, to soak the biscuits but not leave any liquid in the bottom of the dish. Set aside.

Beat together the mascarpone cheese, the egg yolks and the remaining icing sugar. Whisk the egg whites until stiff but not dry, then fold into the cream mixture with 1 of the crumbled chocolate flakes or 25 g (1 oz) of the grated chocolate. Pile the mixture over the coffee-soaked biscuits and smooth the top down. Sprinkle the remaining chocolate over the cream mixture and put in the fridge until ready to serve.

MASCARPONE CHEESE

● This is a slightly sweet cream cheese from Italy which is readily available now on all supermarket cheese or dairy counters. It's very rich, being made from full cream, unlike ricotta and other similar cheeses.

● It's used in Italy for all kinds of puddings, though very rarely for savoury dishes. It mixes with fruit to make very good fruit fool, it's used as a filling for cakes and gateaux, and is sometimes served, rather like ice-cream, to melt over hot Panettone or fruit cake.

Mascarpone Cheese

CRAFTY INGREDIENT

By their very nature, most tarts take a little longer than the 30 minutes we've prescribed for all the recipes in this book. Fortunately, there are a few crafty ways around this problem and the availability of ready-made pastry and pastry cases helps a lot. Biscuits, however, being small and light, cook sufficiently quickly to fit the bill. They are also something that very few people make at home, which is a pity as they're very easy and are something that children can help with and enjoy eating. They are also much better than any shop-bought version, as they tend to have more flavour and less sugar. I've included three kinds for you here, crispy and chewy, and a few ideas for making an instant but quite spectacular French-style tart.

As a small afterthought, it's worth considering using some rather old-fashioned English techniques that benefit from the availability of ready-prepared pastry cases. The traditional jam tart, made on a large scale, is lovely. Use one of the new and very much fruitier conserves — raspberry or apricot or even something more exotic than that — poured into a partly cooked pastry case, topped with a few slivered almonds and quick-baked. It makes a very simple and delicious teatime treat.

TARTS AND BISCUITS

Blueberry and Lemon Biscuits

These are a Transatlantic flavour – the combination of the texture of the dried blueberries and the sharpness of the lemon makes some very interesting and quite large biscuits. They are so easy that they can be made almost immediately when unexpected guests arrive, but, as with many biscuits, they benefit from being allowed to cool properly before eating.

time

30 mins

Makes 24

225 g (8 oz) butter
150 g (5 oz) caster sugar
2 egg yolks
275 g (10 oz) self-raising flour
grated rind of 1 lemon
50 g (2 oz) dried blueberries

Pre-heat the oven to 190°C/375°F/Gas 5.

Using an electric mixer, mix together the butter and sugar until pale. Beat in the egg yolks, flour and lemon rind. When the mixture has almost begun to form into a ball, stir in the blueberries.

Divide the dough into 24 balls, flatten these and place on 2 baking trays, allowing plenty of space for spreading. Bake in the oven for 15–20 minutes, until lightly golden. Allow to cool slightly before transferring on to a cooling rack.

DRIED BLUEBERRIES

● These, along with cranberries which have a slightly sharper flavour and redder colour, are new additions to the dried fruit spectrum and can be used almost interchangeably. They make an interesting addition to muesli and to a dried fruit compote (use dried apricots, pears, apples, prunes, and blueberries and Earl Grey tea).

● They're an interesting and tasty alternative to currants in recipes for Christmas puddings and cakes and also make a very good low-fat snack.

TARTS AND BISCUITS

● As with so many ingredients, these have been transformed in order to allow much more rapid use. Dried apricots used to come pretty dry and needed at least 30 minutes soaking , if not overnight. These are succulent enough to use immediately, if you can if you can resist eating them straight out of the packet.

● They make a marvellous Apricot Fool if stewed gently for about 15 minutes, puréed and mixed with Greek yoghurt or thick double cream. They're delicious cut up and added to breakfast cereals and, following a Middle East tradition, make an excellent sauce for lamb stewed gently in a casserole.

Apricot Flapjacks

I've never understood the name flapjacks, because these are not at all the sort of things that can be slapped on to a baking griddle, turned over quickly and eaten. However, the name now indicates a chewy and often fruity biscuit, usually with some oats in the mixture. These make a really substantial cookie with a very rich and fruity aftertaste.

time

30 mins

Makes 16

75 g (3 oz) butter
75 g (3 oz) light brown sugar
1 tablespoon golden syrup
100 g (4 oz) museli
50 g (2 oz) ready-to-eat apricots, chopped

Pre-heat the oven to 190°C/375°F/Gas 5. Line a 20–23 cm (8–9 inch) square cake tin with greaseproof paper.

Put the butter, sugar and syrup in a saucepan and heat until the butter has melted and the sugar has dissolved. Stir in the museli and the apricots. Pour into the prepared cake tin.

Bake in the oven for 20 minutes. Remove from the oven and allow to cool slightly before cutting into 16 squares, removing from tin and serving.

TARTS AND BISCUITS

Apricots
CRAFTY INGREDIENT

It's understandably easy not to bother with dessert wines. For a start, we've lost the habit of drinking them and it somehow seems much harder to put the right wine to the right pudding. Sadly, this is to miss out on one of life's most exquisite and – forgive the pun – sweetest pleasures.

The trick is to match the sweetness of the wine to the sweetness of the pudding. Yes, okay, this isn't quite as straightforward as it sounds – you've got to know how sweet the pudding is going to be and then you have to do some fingers-crossed shopping to hunt down a suitably sweet, or not so sweet, wine companion.

Thank goodness for back labels! A lot of forward-thinking retailers actually tell you in black and white how sweet the wine is: the sweetest wines are numbered at ten, so you can work backwards from there.

As a rule, the kind of wine that goes well with fruit-based puddings needs to be richly sweet with overtones of honey and tropical fruit. Sauternes is the classic but botrytis-affected Riesling or Sémillon from Australia, German Auslese and Late-Harvest Californian Riesling are also spot on.

If all else fails, you can always add a drop of wine to the pudding – brilliantly effective!

The Perfect Pudding Grape

The aromatic, supercharged, freshly-crushed grape sensation of Muscat turned into sweet wine is an irresistible match to a vast array of puddings, even notoriously difficult chocolate desserts which assault most wines.

Muscat de Beaumes-de-Venise or Moscatel de Valencia, thick with raisin, syrup, chunky orange marmalade flavours that linger on and on, are splendid, just like the showy Californian Elysium, brimming over with a striking cocktail of rosehip syrup, sloes and treacle.

One of the most intriguing sweet wine experiences, though, has to be the tantalizingly light, scrumptious, foamy Asti Spumante. Yes, who would have thought it?! This is quite the best all-rounder, echoing the heavenly sweet tastes of every dessert, from the most delicate of fresh fruits to the richest, stodgiest Christmas pudding.

Pear and Redcurrant Sponge Flan

This recipe produces a lovely, succulent pudding, unexpectedly moist and extremely attractive. It's best made when fresh redcurrants are available as frozen ones never seem to have the same physical or flavour appeal. It's quite floppy to serve so make sure you have something like a fish slice or cake slice available to help you move it. Double cream, possibly lightly whipped, goes very well.

time

15 mins

Serves 6

400 g (14 oz) can pear halves in juice (not syrup), drained
3 tablespoons redcurrant jelly
1 large ready-baked sponge flan case
1 punnet redcurrants
1 tablespoon icing sugar

Put 2 pear halves and the redcurrant jelly in a food processor and blend until smooth. Spread the mixture over the base of the sponge. Cut lengthways incisions through the remaining pears at 5mm (¼ inch) intervals, then place in fan shapes, across the base of the sponge. Rinse the redcurrants and, leaving them with their stalks on, dip them into or sprinkle them with the icing sugar. Arrange them in attractive patterns over the pears. The flan can be kept for up to 1 hour before serving.

● These are available in a number of shapes and sizes, both round and oblong.

● I find the oblong one best for the pears but round ones are also a very useful basis for a quick cheesecake or for filling with finely chopped fruit salad, flavoured, perhaps, with a little elderflower syrup before topping with whipped cream.

Sponge Flan
CRAFTY INGREDIENT

TARTS AND BISCUITS

Chocolate Chip Cookies

These biscuits are very easy to make and have the additional benefit of being ideal for children to help with, without adding a lot of time to the preparation. Do let them cool when you've cooked them because the crispness only emerges once the biscuits have had a chance to really cool down.

time

30 mins

Makes 24 biscuits

100 g (4 oz) butter

75 g (3 oz) caster sugar

I egg yolk

150 g (5 oz) self-raising flour

75 g (3 oz) chocolate chips

Pre-heat the oven to 190°C/375°F/Gas 5.

Using an electric mixer, cream together the butter and sugar until pale and fluffy. Beat in the egg and flour and finally the chocolate chips.

Divide the mixture into 24 small balls and place on 2 large baking trays. Using a fork, gently flatten slightly. Bake in the oven for 10–15 minutes, until lightly golden. Allow to cool slightly before transferring on to a wire cooling rack.

CHOCOLATE CHIPS

● These come in both milk and plain chocolate – I much prefer the plain chocolate ones. In addition to being used in cookies, they make a very interesting addition to chocolate cakes, adding an unexpected bite, crunch and texture. I add them to the cake mixture itself or you can add them to chocolate icing.

● I like them in Chocolate Mousse, the kind you make with melted chocolate and egg. They also make an extremely pleasant addition to a mint ice-cream.

Instant Apple Tarts

I invented this unlikely proposition for a cookery demonstration at the Good Food Show in Birmingham where we were trying to do a traditional Sunday lunch in 30 minutes. In fact they proved to be the sensation of the show as they are easy to make and, if not quite instant, they don't take very long. You need the sort of tin that's used to bake individual Yorkshire puddings.

● This is one of the latest developments in the wonderful saga of readily available pastries. Not only is the pastry made for you but it's also rolled out as well. It's very rare that it's rolled out exactly to fit your tins, but it is an enormous blessing and involves virtually no work at all.

● You can use it to line full-sized tarts for quiches, to cover savoury dishes such as Steak and Kidney Pie, and cut it into a lattice with one of the ready-made lattice cutters to make an Apple or Mincemeat Tart. The uses are endless and it's one of the great inventions of our time.

Serves 4

time

25 mins

225 g (8 oz) pre-rolled shortcrust pastry
2 large eating apples
50 g (2 oz) butter
25 g (1 oz) caster sugar
2 tablespoons apricot jam

Pre-heat the oven to 190°C/375°F/Gas 5. Use the pastry to line the bases of a 4-portion Yorkshire pudding tin and prick all over with a fork. Bake in the oven for about 10 minutes until golden brown.

Meanwhile, core, but do not peel, the apples and cut each into 6 wedges. Melt the butter in a frying pan, add the apples and cook gently for 4–5 minutes, until golden and slightly softened. Add the sugar and stir to coat the apple wedges.

Arrange the apple wedges in pretty shapes in the cooked pastry cases. Spread with the apricot jam, then return to the oven for about 5 minutes for the jam to form a glaze. Serve hot or cold.

Pre-rolled
Shortcrust Pastry
CRAFTY INGREDIENT

TARTS AND BISCUITS

French Apricot Flan

French Apricot Flan is one of the great classics of French cookery and used to be the basis on which restaurants were judged, along with their omelettes, plain roast chicken and wonderful bread. It is an apparently complex recipe but made very simple by two key ingredients, ready made and readily available now in our supermarkets and stores. If you decide to make this and keep it for a while, don't be tempted to put it in the fridge because everything goes soggy.

time

30 mins

Serves 6–8

1 tablespoon cornflour

2 tablespoons milk

2 eggs, separated

1 x 400 g (14 oz) tub ready-made fresh cream custard

1 ready-cooked 20 cm (8 inch) plain or sweet flan case

420 g (14½ oz) can apricots halves in juice, drained

4 tablespoons apricot jam

Blend the cornflour with the milk until smooth. Beat the egg yolks into the custard, then beat in the cornflour mixture. Pour into a saucepan and bring slowly to the boil, stirring continuously. Do not allow the mixture to bubble once it has come to the boil. Pour the slightly cooked mixture into the prepared pastry case. Top with the drained apricot halves, cut side down, as close together as possible.

Heat the apricot jam in a saucepan, push through a sieve, then spread carefully over the apricots, allowing it to run down the sides and eventually coat the custard as well. Leave for at least 10 minutes to set. The flan can be kept for up to 2 hours at room temperature before serving.

FRESH CUSTARD

● This is something that's only recently arrived in the chill cabinets and is great. It's properly made custard with cream, sugar and eggs and far more delicious than the powdered, bright yellow variety. It is excellent with pies and all kinds of puddings but, as used in this method, also turns into an instant crème pâtissère, that gorgeous cream that French bakers and pie-makers use to line their fruit pies.

● It's good for trifles and as the basis for dishes that have a custard component, like Bakewell Tart, where you stir almonds as well as egg yolks into the mixture before baking it in a pastry case.

Custard
CRAFTY INGREDIENT

Oz WINE Wine Doctor

Is it true that red wine reduces the risk of coronary heart disease and strokes?

Yes! Indeed, it's considered the thinking person's health drink. A moderate daily dose of alcohol in any form is positively beneficial to health, acting as an instant anti-coagulant, lowering 'bad' cholesterol and raising 'good' cholesterol. However, red wine provides much more than just alcohol. Grape skins contain antioxidant flavonoids which are thought to be active in disease prevention and because red wine is created by macerating the skins in grape juice, the flavonoids are retained.

How many glasses of wine can I safely drink a week?

One small glass of wine (125ml/4fl.oz.) equals one unit and current UK Government guidelines stand at 28 units per week for men and 21 for women, which are a reasonable safety first guide. Ideally, we should space out consumption of daily units over the course of 24 hours. What you shouldn't do is to save them all up for one huge drinking session at the end of the week and reckon you're still within safe limits – apart from the hangover, bingeing is definitely NOT good for the body.

Is there a wine that reduces the risk of a hangover?

There are plenty of low alcohol and non-alcoholic wines around but, to be honest, while this shouldn't have to mean low taste, most are pretty frightful and bear no resemblance to the real thing.

Another word of warning. In practice, wines described as alcohol-free or de-alcoholized can contain up to 0.05% alcohol. In spritzers, reduced alcohol or low alcohol wines, the alcohol content can be as much as 5.5% – potentially more intoxicating than some beers and lagers!! The message here is to look carefully at the small print.

Some people suffer more from drinking red wine – this is understandable as more chemical compounds are leached out of the grape skins. Try drinking one glass of water to each glass of wine - this has a nice diluting effect.

How do you open a bottle of fizz safely?

Damon Hill makes it look easy but he's used to big tyres – the pressure in a fizz bottle is exactly the same as a London double-decker bus tyre! Damon is also accustomed to speed – a fizz cork is capable of flying out at an alarming 60 miles per hour, a bit slow by Grand Prix standards, but pretty dangerous nevertheless. Keep the cork under control – turn the bottle and the cork simultaneously and avoid pointing the bottle at your best friend!

I occasionally find something in wine that looks like sugar crystals. What are they and do they harm the wine - or me?!

Don't worry! These small deposits are caused by the precipitation of tartaric acid. They are tasteless, don't affect flavour and are totally harmless – to you and the wine!

Is it true that screw-top bottles are better for wine?

Thanks to the cork-contaminating compound 2,4,6-trichloroanisole (TCA), as much as a disgraceful eight per cent of all wines are ruined by a truly offensive dirty-birdcage-lined-with-mouldy-socks smell and taste. If every wine bottle had a screw-top or synthetic cork – and there's no logical reason why they shouldn't - this problem would be eradicated.

How long will wine keep after opening?

Young, modern wines can keep for days simply with the cork slammed back in the bottle. Reds deteriorate more quickly than whites but whites, to be honest, can keep for weeks in the fridge with minimal deterioration, the cold temperature arresting most of the decaying effect of exposure to air.

My weight-reducing diet bans wine! Can I cheat and have a glass of dry white?! How many calories are there in a glass of wine?

About the same as a banana! Red or white, a small glass (125ml/4fl.oz.) contains roughly 120 calories. I'm afraid to say it but, if you really want to thin those thighs, alcohol has to be sacrificed! It's the alcohol that piles on the pounds - the relative sweetness is negligible.

Index